THE WISDOM OF GROUP DECISIONS

100 PRINCIPLES AND PRACTICAL TIPS

FOR COLLABORATION

Craig Freshley

The Wisdom of Group Decisions

100 Principles and Practical Tips for Collaboration

Copyright © 2010 Craig Freshley

Manufactured in the United States of America

Published by
Good Group Decisions
98 Maine Street
Brunswick, ME 04011
www.GoodGroupDecisions.com

*Dedicated to Dana
whose easy-going tolerance,
laughter, and sunny disposition
remind me to lighten up.*

CONTENTS

PREFACE

We need new and better ways of making decisions together. As a society and in the many groups that we all belong to, we have made poor decisions that have threatened our future.

If we believe that we have some hand in our destiny, that the decisions we make together today affect how things will be tomorrow, then we should invest in making good decisions. Whether in a family, a company, community group, or country, better collaboration results in better decisions for more people for years to come.

Linear decision making (someone in charge making decisions for others in a hierarchical framework) is a hallmark of western civilization. We have built empires through competition and conquest. While linear decision making is sometimes effective, more creative and sustainable decisions emerge with collaborative decision making. While linear decisions may be swift, collaborative decisions serve us better over the long run.

Our popular culture works against collaborative decision making; it encourages us to put ourselves first and pursue personal desires at all cost. Conventional decision-making ethics encourage personal gain, condone borrowing against the future, and promote the notion that there are winners and losers. As a result, our world is rife with disagreement, frustration, low self-esteem and greed.

While a few individuals win, our communities lose. Our neighborhoods, cities, countries, corporations and other institutions fall far short of what they could be. Our Earth increasingly lacks the resources to keep up with this greed.

Collaborative decision making is a key part of every solution.

I have worked the halls of state legislatures, the board rooms of corporate headquarters, and the folding metal chairs of church basements. I have bachelor's degrees in political science and philosophy and a master's degree in public policy and management. For eleven years I worked at the Maine state capital doing public policy development. I live in a cohousing community that strives to make decisions by consensus and I have served on and chaired several nonprofit boards and committees. I am a Quaker. I have made notes for this book for many years.

These are not the only Principles and Tips for making good group decisions, or the only way to organize them. This is just one attempt to advance our collective thinking on how to make better decisions together. This is just one set of frames snatched out of the blurry video of human evolution, a few snapshots that I happen to like.

I invite you to develop your own pictures of how to make better group decisions. Share with me and others your ideas about how to make better decisions for our future. We need all the help we can get. All contributions welcome.

Craig Freshley
Carrabassett Valley, Maine
July, 2009

ACKNOWLEDGMENTS

Hundreds of people have contributed to and supported my work through the years for which I am very grateful. Special thanks to Jim Martin for early review of this text, Darcy Rollins Saas for copy editing, Nick Humez for indexing, Cynthia Brownell for illustrations, Jennifer Cigno for cover design, Elizabeth Andrews for the back cover photo, and Nancy Poes for the painting on the front cover. Thanks to Dana and Sara. A special thanks to my wife Carol.

INTRODUCTION

WHAT IS A *GOOD* GROUP DECISION?

When good decisions are made, things are better over the long run for many people; problems are solved and/or good things are created. Also, good decisions bring peace; people get along with each other better. Given these benefits, good decisions endure over time. They are not quickly over-turned.

Good decisions are more likely when many people are involved in the decision-making process. Good decisions require good collaboration.

Collaboration is like curves, circles, and cycles. One person deciding is like lines, squares, and steps.

Linear decision making is when someone in charge makes decisions for others within a hierarchical framework. It is how most decisions are made today. Throughout corporations, governments, and nonprofits, individuals are empowered to rule over specific domains. This is sometimes a very effective and efficient way to make decisions, but not always.

Collaborative decision making is most appropriate when the decision (or lack of decision) affects many people in a significant way for a long time, *and* when there is sufficient willingness, time, and other resources to support a collaborative process.

When these conditions exist, collaborative decision making is highly effective, even magical.

Caroline Estes, from whom I and many others have learned about collaborative decision making, told me, "Each person has a piece of the truth. We make our best decisions when we put all our truths together." I once saw a sign in a board room that said: "No one in this room is smarter than all of us."

When we take the time to really consider alternative perspectives and alternative solutions, creative and lasting decisions emerge. Not only that, we feel good about working with each other to implement the decision.

FOR BIG IMPACTS

Let's imagine the range of ways groups make decisions. Sometimes, one person decides on behalf of everyone else in the group. Other times, most of the group decides for everyone. And sometimes, every group member participates in the decision.

One Decider   Majority Rule   Whole Group Decides

One decider, majority rule, and *whole group decides* simply describe the end points and middle of a colorful spectrum of all the ways groups make decisions.

Implementing a plan is better suited to single person or small group, toward the left end of the spectrum. Making a plan (planning) is better done with a larger group, toward the right end. On the field of battle the commander decides (left end) and everyone obeys—plans are swiftly implemented. The foreign policy (right end) that guides a battle is made by the United States Senate with a wide array of input—plans are made by many.

Short-lived decisions are well suited to single deciders while long-lived decisions best involve many. Deciding the design of a new town hall—a building expected to last hundreds of years—should involve many stakeholders. Deciding what paper to use in the photo copier in the new town hall is a single-person decision. Decisions with a limited sphere of impact are good for single deciders or small groups but when a decision affects hundreds of people, or thousands or millions of people, then hundreds, thousands, or millions of people should be involved.

When groups use highly collaborative methods for relatively small decisions the result is often frustration and gross inefficiency. This is why collaborative decision making has a reputation for being cumbersome: it is often misapplied. Groups that try for consensus on every decision get terribly stuck.

On the other hand, when single decider methods are applied to significant decisions with long-term and broad impact, benefits accrue to a few at the expense of many. Big decisions made by small groups of leaders tend to perpetuate their power and compromise the health and well-being of the group as a whole. Linear decision making by society leaders has resulted in environmental degradation and gross social inequities.

Organizations and societies that strive to be both collaborative and individually decisive use a *tree of collaboration* rather than a *chain of command*.

In the trunk of the tree of collaboration are the core beliefs that bring us together, the core reasons why we are a group. The trunk is our foundation: our mission, values, strategic plan, and basic operating rules. Branches are major areas of activity, each governed by a different yet connected group. Faster, less-inclusive decisions are made here. Branches are programs, agencies, divisions, departments. Most decisions on behalf of the organization are made in the leaves and twigs—by individuals and small groups.

We trust people throughout the organization to make decisions on behalf of the organization because they participated in making the big decisions about mission, values, plan, and rules. Each front line decision maker has "bought in" to the bigger picture and can be trusted to make aligned decisions.

In the chain of command, each link is connected in a line to another yet each link is physically separate. They rattle. In the tree of collaboration, the same sap runs through the whole tree. Each leaf and bud is genetically connected.

ATTITUDES AND ACTIONS

There are many "how to" guides that provide rules, guidelines, and steps that a group should follow to make good decisions. Robert's Rules of Order is the best known for majority-rule groups such as legislatures and boards of directors. Yet we have all seen groups follow steps perfectly and make bad decisions.

Good group decisions rely on more than good rules and good facilitation. Good collaboration depends on the good attitudes that participants bring and on the good actions that they take.

Certain attitudes and beliefs do not support good group decisions. When I believe that I am better than others and that I know best, I am not a good collaborative decision maker. In fact, I get in the way of others trying to collaborate. I am not a good collaborative decision maker when I am closed-minded, when I feel sorry for myself or victimized, when I feel entitled, when I am skeptical, apathetic, or negative.

Good group decisions require that participants have certain attitudes, values, and ways of looking at the world and their place in it. I am most helpful to collaborative decision making when I am humble, when I believe that the next great idea could come from anywhere—not just me. I contribute best when I believe that there is good in everyone, when I am optimistic, enthusiastic, and want to genuinely give to the group without any conditions or resentments. Good group decisions require the fundamental belief that what is best for the group is most important.

All talk and no action is just talk. To make the world better, whatever world we are talking and deciding about, we act. Good collaborative decision makers can be trusted to follow through. We give life to our group decisions when we do what we said we would do.

Good group decisions require that we try things on, that we try things out before deciding. We take action in little steps and learn from them incrementally. Good group decisions require courage and leadership.

People who are most helpful to making good group decisions have a willingness to take action combined with an attitude of humility.

PROCESS FROM SUBSTANCE

In one-decider and majority-rule decision making the deciders not only decide on the substance, they control the process. The king decides who comes before him and the king serves as judge and jury. In majority-rule groups the majority party decides the agenda and sets the rules for participation. In these ways, single deciders and majorities manage and adjust the process to serve their own interests.

To make truly collaborative decisions we want full participation from all perspectives. We each have a piece of the truth. Collaborative decision-making groups often request a neutral third party, sometimes called a facilitator, to manage the group process. The facilitator does not have a preferred outcome and uses techniques to encourage widespread and creative participation.

We each have a piece of the truth.

Collaborative does not mean casual. Good collaborative processes are structured and scheduled. When groups are well practiced in collaborative decision making and well facilitated, the process is highly efficient.

When participants are empowered to focus on the substance of the decision and a designated facilitator is focused on the process of decision making, both substance and process are better. Skilled facilitation brings efficiency and full participation. Not having to watchdog the process, participants bring their full creativity.

LIFE LONG RESULTS

When we analyze a decision's entire life cycle, from when it is first decided for as long as people are doing things because of it, we see the virtues of collaborative decision making. Success is not measured by how long the decision took to make, but how well the decision endures.

Making a decision collaboratively and arriving at full-group consensus may be hard but implementing it is a breeze. Every person is likely to understand the decision and help implement it. Further, for a long time to come, many people remember the process, the reasons for the decision, and defend the decision.

When a majority makes a decision, there is a minority out there trying to change the decision and/or hamper its implementation. There is never lasting peace between majorities and minorities.

When a dictator decides something, he must be able to enforce it. Decision making is a breeze; implementing decisions is often violent.

As a rule, the more people who help make and agree with a decision, the fewer people likely to stand in the way of its implementation. The more collaborative the process, the longer the decision is likely to last.

Making peace is harder than making war. Fighting with each other is often easier than talking with each other. Fully inclusive and collaborative decisions are very hard compared to individual or majority decisions. Collaborative decision making requires us to listen carefully, consider all perspectives, sit through a lot of meetings. Collaborative decisions take longer than individual or majority decisions. They cost more.

Yet collaborative decisions are usually worth much more over the long run, over the life of the decision.

WHY GROUP DECISIONS?

FOR THE EARTH

The Earth needs recovery. Perhaps we are at step one. Just now, many of us are accepting that we have a problem, really, a big problem.

In the United States we have become addicted to the extraordinary benefits that capitalism and empire building have brought. We have been unable to resist the temptations of cars, gadgets, media thrills and conveniences. And why should we? The well of ever-new, yet affordable, consumer products has kept pumping since the industrial revolution, and we have kept drinking.

Using up resources and consuming oil is fun but there are serious side effects:

The warmest year on record was 2007. The World Meteorological Organization ranks 1998–2007 as the warmest decade on record.[1]

The number of threatened species reached 16,928 in 2008. At least 869 species are known to be extinct.[2]

Almost half of Earth's original forest cover is gone, much of it destroyed within the past three decades.[3]

In 2008, on the day declared by the United Nations as *International Day of Peace*, there were 30 ongoing wars in the world.[4]

We are coming to terms with the fact that our behavior is not sustainable. If we keep doing things this way, things will get worse. Climate change is the defining human development issue of our generation.[5] It's not someone's fault. It's not something we asked for. We need to simply accept it and take steps to address it.

We stand at a critical moment in Earth's history.

Joanna Macy has said, "A revolution is underway because people are realizing that our needs can be met without destroying our world. We have the technical knowledge, the communication tools, and material resources to grow enough food, ensure clean air and water, and meet rational energy needs. Future generations, if there is a livable world for them, will look back at the epochal transition we are making to a life-sustaining society. And they may well call this the time of the Great Turning. It is happening now."[6]

In a book called *The Great Turning*, David Korten explains how an *empire* mentality has dominated our culture for 5,000 years; leaders have sought material wealth at the expense of other people. The result has been widespread oppression and poverty among most of the world's people and dangerous, wasteful plunder of most of the world's natural resources. [7]

To save ourselves, argues Korten, we must shift to a culture of "Earth Community." The term is used in the preamble of the Earth Charter, a document crafted by thousands of people from throughout the world around the time of the 1992 Earth Summit: "We stand at a critical moment in Earth's history, a time when humanity must choose its future. As the world becomes increasingly interdependent and fragile, the future at once holds great peril and great promise. To move forward we must recognize that, in the midst of a magnificent diversity of cultures and life forms, we are one human family and one Earth Community with a common destiny. We must join together to bring forth a sustainable global society founded on respect for nature, universal human rights, economic justice, and a culture of peace. Towards this end, it is imperative that we, the peoples of Earth, declare our responsibility to one another, to the greater community of life, and to future generations."[8]

Chapter 3 of the Earth Charter specifically calls us to "...build democratic societies that are just, participatory, sustainable, and peaceful." Principle 13 calls for "...inclusive participation in decision making."[9]

Similarly, the tenth principle of the United Nation's Agenda 21—a program to promote sustainability globally, nationally, and locally—calls for states to "...facilitate and encourage public awareness and participation by making information widely available." It says, "...environmental issues are best handled with the participation of all concerned citizens, at the relevant level."[10]

We must make decisions in new ways. Old ways, mostly small groups of men pursuing their empire-building interests, have resulted in bad decisions. We have used up our natural resources and we have degraded our environment to the point of crisis. We continue to make war on each other in family and workplace skirmishes and in huge genocidal conflicts.

Poor decision making is not entirely responsible for the mess we are in. More collaborative decision making is not the sole solution. It is *part* of the solution, an important part of the Great Turning.

When we apply the Principles and Tips in this book we look further into the future and beyond our own immediacy, in all directions. The Principles and Tips in this book encourage inclusion, tolerance, understanding, and compassion—all things that help make peace on Earth. When we are grateful, open, patient, respectful, and humble, we make decisions that are lighter on Earth.

Making decisions more collaboratively sounds like we are nice to each other, tolerant, inclusive. It seems like the right thing to do from a moral perspective. It is.

It is also the right thing to do from an economic perspective, from a practical perspective. Collaborative decision making is an investment. The sacrifice is immediate and the benefit comes over time. It takes more time than just deciding by yourself. It takes the time and effort of many people in your organization. Yet for many decisions, investing in collaboration is absolutely worthwhile.

Collaboration outperforms competition in many institutional settings. Alfie Kohn points out that, while a competitive attitude may help you *beat the other guys*, you might have achieved even more if you were not concerned with that objective.[11] Collaboration is about achievement whereas competition is about subordination. Further, he argues, collaboration is often more efficient. Competition, by its nature, requires more resources; it is often duplicative.

Collaboration results in more creative decisions. Like new life, new ideas are born out of the connection between two or more previously unrelated ideas. The more people working on a decision, the greater the likelihood of two or more wild ideas merging into a great one.

Group decisions breed innovation.

Group decisions breed innovation. It is innovation that propels companies, nonprofits, and governments forward by leaps and bounds. It is innovation that solves the toughest problems. The more collaboration, the more innovation.

A related benefit: more chance of identifying unintended consequences (unforeseen negative impacts). When we take the time to hear the concerns and ideas of *all* the groups of people affected by a decision, we are likely to reveal almost all potential impacts, intended and unintended. Unintended consequences present huge liabilities for organizations and for our society. Collaboration reduces unintended consequences.

Another economic benefit of collaborative decision making comes from the unity among members. People who are asked to take part in decision making, who work in a culture of collaboration, feel a sense of belonging, teamwork, and desire to accomplish tasks for the good of the group. They want to help implement the things they helped to decide. Collaborative participants want to be efficient and productive.

Collaboration creates new wealth. When building empires, new wealth is created for an organization at the expense of other organizations and other people. Wealth is brought in from outside the organization. When collaborating, the wealth of the participants (not just money but all that is contributed) creates new wealth from within. Collaborative organizations create their own capital from the synergy of their people.

FOR YOU

For me, participating in collaborative decisions has taught me about myself, brought me closer to others, and brought me peace.

Participating in collaborative decisions requires us to speak our truth. To do that, we must know our truth. Deciding things in collaboration with others has pushed me to know my own truths, decide what I really care about.

It also teaches me about others. When I take time to understand the rationale for others' perspectives I am more tolerant of them. When I am open-minded, I appreciate the beauty, talent, and ideas of others. The more we decide together, the more I learn about my fellows.

Collaborative decision making lets me let go. Knowing that I share in the decision with others, I do not have to hold the whole thing. I do my part and let go of the rest. There are others holding other pieces.

Collaborative decision making reminds me to be humble, that I do not always know best. Actually, I rarely know best. I trust the wisdom *of the group* and this releases me from the burden of having to decide *for the group*. It brings me peace. I trust that collaborative decision making will bring benefits for you, too.

ABOUT THE PRINCIPLES AND TIPS

These Principles and Tips are meant for you to know and apply in your own way. Relate them to your own experience. There is something personal about them. Groups are made of individuals. The behavior of a group as a whole stems from what the individual members do. These Principles and Tips are designed to help *you* help your group.

None of the Principles or Tips is more important than any other. At any given moment in any given place, one of them may be most important.

The Principles and Tips are not rules, but guidelines. There are exceptions to every one. Hopefully, most of the time, they guide where there are no rules or when our present rules do not work.

The Principles and Tips are represented by simple headings and short sentences; few words intended as doorways to more learning. The Tips are like tips of icebergs with a lot below the surface.

CONNECTED MAPS

The Principles and Tips are extremely interconnected; reading one brings others to mind. None can be practiced without at the same time practicing others. Not one stands on its own. They are interlocking; inseparable.

You are invited to skip around as you read. This is not a novel with a plot that gets increasingly revealed from start to finish. Rather, this is more like an atlas with page after page of maps.

The Principles and Tips in this book, like maps in an atlas, are at different scales. Some maps are of city streets, some of countries, some of continents; you are expected to jump back and forth from big picture to detailed picture, from meticulous to context.

Like maps at different scales.

As you explore the pages of this collaborative decision-making atlas, you will see that not all Principles and Tips are relevant to every situation. Indeed, the solution to many group decision challenges is found in just one or two of the Principles and Tips.

To start, pick a topic that you recognize, like a place you know of in an atlas. Explore and move on from there.

WAYS WITHOUT END

The word *way* means *method* or *technique*, and it also means *path*, *route*, or *direction*. I do not offer a singular set of methods or paths that will lead a group to perfect decisions. I offer general direction. It is up to each individual and group to decide exactly how to go, as they go. The way is often vague and changing.

Not only that, collaborative decision making is a way with no end, like a circle. It is more like an art gallery than a football game, more like a wandering exploration of perspectives and emotions than a focused effort to gain ground towards a goal. Circles have no starting place and art galleries have no end zones. Start anywhere. Don't end. Achieve your dreams along the way.

PRINCIPLES
AND
PRACTICAL TIPS

ACT AS IF

In principle, making good group decisions is really hard, a lot harder than making bad decisions. Getting along with each other and making peaceful, lasting decisions takes a lot of practice.

Act is part of the word *practice*. We don't get better without action. We do things poorly until we can do them well. It is not so important that we succeed, but that we try.

Practical Tip: We practice the principles of good group decisions as best we can. For guidance we ask ourselves, "What would a peaceful person do?" We don't just talk about how to make peaceful decisions, or read about it, or think about it—we practice making good group decisions. Most of us are not very good peacemakers but when we try to act as if we are, our world becomes more peaceful.

We do things poorly
until we can do them well.

AGENDA SETTING ACCESS

In principle, if we are a group of relative equals, deciding how we are going to spend our time together should be a group decision, or at least the group should decide the agenda-setting process. Further, every group member should understand the agenda-setting process and have access to it.

In many groups, agenda setting is closely guarded by the majority or the chair and is often used to limit opposition. In most political systems, being able to control the agenda is a huge source of power.

Practical Tip: Establish an open and fair process for setting meeting agendas and make sure everyone knows the process. To maximize creativity, air all perspectives, and share power; make it relatively easy for any new issue or idea to get at least a brief hearing.

Some groups reserve a special time in every agenda where anyone can raise any issue—sometimes called "open forum"—and then the issue might be sent to committee or placed on a future agenda. Some groups vote or consent to approve the proposed agenda at the start of every meeting.

In any case, agenda setting is not trivial and if the agenda-setting process is not formalized and widely understood in your group, it is likely limiting your creativity and your ability to make good group decisions.

In principle, the same formality is required to change an agreement as to make an agreement. For instance, if an agreement is made in a group meeting and properly documented, no member of the group should assume that the agreement has changed or act in ways contrary to the agreement until the agreement is changed in a group meeting and properly documented.

Group agreements often get ignored over time and people come to think it is okay to behave contrary to what was agreed to. The problem with this is that expectations become unclear, especially for newcomers. People are navigating according to different maps—some written, some imagined—and many people are lost. There is inefficiency, frustration, and resentment.

Practical Tip: Make group agreements with a degree of formality and write them down (in meeting notes or otherwise). When it becomes apparent that people are behaving contrary to an agreement there are two choices: Point out how behavior is contrary to an agreement (people may simply not know) and, if contrary behavior continues, enforce the agreement by imposing consequences on violators. Or, formally change the agreement to be in line with behavior. Things change and sometimes agreements need to change, fine.

Ignoring, condoning, or practicing disagreeable behavior is not a choice; not if you are striving for harmony, productivity, and efficiency in your group.

ALTERNATIVE SOLUTIONS

In principle, considering alternative solutions makes for better decisions. Exploring alternatives results in one or more of the following:

1. Builds faith in the leading option. We get to see that the leading option really is the best among alternatives.

2. Leads to a new, better solution.

3. Reveals that we do not have a clear handle on the problem. Posing alternative solutions pushes us to clearly define the problem that we are trying to solve.

When we invite alternatives and genuinely consider them, it also builds credibility among those we ask and increases chances of their participation in the solution.

Practical Tip: Even when you think you have the right answer, pose alternatives. Consider, "What are some other ways to approach this? How else could we get the job done? How else could we solve the problem?" Be wildly creative. Be hypothetical. Like a child posing dolls or trucks, be imaginative. Decide after you have posed and considered alternative solutions.

In principle, there are three ways of knowing about something or someone: what we know, what we don't know, and what we think we know...and it's usually what we think we know that gets us in trouble. When we assume things, we gamble; the bigger the assumption, the bigger the risk.

In any endeavor based on assumptions we can absolutely count on some of them giving way, like support timbers under a house collapsing. Some assumptions may hold for a long time, some almost forever, but most will collapse at a bad time and cause damage. When we make decisions based on facts and when we acknowledge all that we do not know, the long-term outcomes are better.

Practical Tip: When analyzing a situation write down what you know, what you don't know, and what you assume. Naming assumptions is key. Want to play it safe? Don't make assumptions. How? Catch yourself making assumptions.

In principle, 90 percent of disease prevention and curing is done at home and in families. We all practice health care. We help each other eat well, get rest, and we take care of each other when sick. Only sometimes do we see a doctor or some other medical professional. Same with collaborative decisions: 90 percent of conflict prevention and resolution is done at home and in families. We help each other see things differently, we settle arguments, and we offer compassion and advice to those in conflict. Similarly, we all do the work of collaborative decisions in our jobs and in community groups. Only sometimes do we hire a facilitator or mediator.

Practical Tip: Just as I take 90 percent responsibility for my own health and my family's health, I take 90 percent responsibility for peace and good decision making in the groups I belong to. To do it well I educate myself about what really works, beyond wives' tales, and I try to actually do what I learn. Also, I self-diagnose. I ask, "What did I do today that contributed to a more peaceful world?" And, "How could I do better?"

Like a sick person visualizing themselves as healthy, I try to see myself as a peacemaker. I don't need a license to practice.

In principle, when things are not right, a natural instinct is to want someone else to do something different or to want a policy to be different, but rarely are these the best solutions. It is easy to think my problem would be solved if only you would change. It is easy to think that the law or policy is wrong, rather than me. Sometimes laws or other people's attitudes or behaviors need to change, but it is often most effective to change my own attitudes or behaviors.

Practical Tip: Before going to the leaders of my group and suggesting a policy change, or before going to another group member and suggesting they should change, I ask, "What is my part in this? What can I change about my own attitude or behavior to fix things?" If I have answered those questions, acted on the answers, and still things aren't right, then I ask my group or fellow group member to consider a change.

When we work to change a governing policy to fix an isolated problem, it can be hugely inefficient for many people. When we work to change the behaviors of others without willingness to change ourselves, it can take huge amounts of energy and result in damaged relations.

To help the efficiency of collaborative decisions the first question is not, "What should he or she or they do to make things better?" but rather, "What am I going to do to make things better?"

It is easy to think that my problem would be solved if only you would change.

CARROTS ARE BETTER THAN STICKS

In principle, you can get a donkey to move forward in two ways: entice her in front with a carrot or hit her from behind with a stick. Carrots are rewards, incentives, appreciation, and—the most compelling—visions of how things can be better. Sticks are punishments, criticisms, and—the most destructive—defeatism, pessimism, and a sense that things are hopelessly bad.

When motivated by sticks we are generally resentful, in pain, and when the stick is gone our motivation disappears. When we are motivated by compelling visions, it's called *inspiration* and it fuels our forward movement from within.

Practical Tip: Develop, nurture, and share visions of things being better. Inspire! Rather than catch someone doing something wrong and criticize them, catch someone doing something right and praise them. Rather than focus on what bad things might happen if decided a certain way, focus on what good things might happen if decided differently. Rather than complain about all that is wrong, give thanks for all that is right. Pass the carrots, please.

In principle, the cause of most conflict is misunderstanding. The parties don't have the same facts, same experience, same perspective, and don't fully appreciate how someone else could see it differently.

A second cause of conflict is fundamental difference of values. This is where the parties understand the facts and each other but they simply have different values. For example, one person believes in Jesus as savior, another does not. Each person's beliefs are deeply rooted and not easily changed.

Third, parties are in conflict because of some outside issue, something that has nothing to do with the immediate issue at hand. The conflict might be because of some incident between the parties that happened years ago and has never been dealt with or because of a mental disorder, an irrational fear, or an addiction that is influencing someone's judgment or behavior. An outside issue is preventing one or more people from seeing or acting clearly.

Practical Tip: When conflicts arise, work first to develop shared understanding. Talk, listen, express truth, learn, be open-minded, let go, ponder, talk some more.

If differing values are the cause, identify the values you have in common. Identify your common goals. See how you believe in similar things but have different ways of acting on them. Work on the things you agree on and let go of the rest, for now.

If a debilitating outside issue is at play, peace will only come about if the issue is dealt with. If it is your issue, deal with it, seek help, do the personal work. If the issue is not dealt with by the parties, an outside authority must be invoked to make and enforce a decision.

CHANGE OR ACCEPT

In principle, when I am in conflict with others in my group or troubled by a difficult circumstance, and I want relief, I have basically two choices: I can either work to change things for the better or I can work to accept things as they are. Both paths require effort on my part. Idle complaints, criticisms, or gossip will not really help things and will likely make things worse.

And most things, it's helpful to keep in mind, I probably can't change. The only thing I really have power over is my own beliefs and behaviors. If I changed these, would it ease the conflict?

Practical Tip: When in conflict, draw a circle around yourself. Draw it so that inside the circle are the things you can change and outside the circle are the things you cannot:

1. Define the circle of things within your control.

2. Work to change things within the circle.

3. Let go of all that's outside the circle.

In other words: define your part; take responsibility for improving your part; do not take on other parts.

Work inside the circle—addressing the things you can change—is all about action. It's about doing things differently.

Work outside the circle—the things you can't change—is all about acceptance. It's about seeing things differently.

The only thing I really have power over
is my own beliefs and behaviors.

In principle, making good decisions together as a group requires three key ingredients: It requires good decision-making processes to be sure, but it also depends on the attitudes of individual participants and the actions they take. A group's decision-making process is only part of what makes for good decisions.

Practical Tip: Use individual conversations to address individual issues. Realize that for many problems encountered by your group, the problem is not the group's process. Problems are most often the result of individual beliefs or behaviors.

We often try to adjust group process as a backdoor way to address someone's different beliefs or to get someone to change their behavior. Changing group policy often seems easier than having a one-on-one conversation, but one-on-one conversations save group time and energy.

In principle, not every task is best suited to the full group and not every topic is interesting to every group member. When groups establish committees—sub-groups of people focused on specific activities—it brings focused attention to issues, draws on the enthusiasm of those most interested, and frees the full group for higher-level business.

Committee members often volunteer for service although they may be formally appointed by the full group, chair, or boss. Standing committees—such as an organization's finance committee or program committee— have ongoing, often annual, responsibilities. Ad hoc committees are established for specific purposes and go out of business once that purpose is achieved. Ad hoc committees are often asked to research something and make recommendations.

Committees work best with written mandates and willing participants.

Practical Tip: When tasking a sub-group, write a mandate. What are you asking the committee to do? What is within the scope of work and what is out of bounds? When do you expect to hear from the committee? Don't shy from drafting a committee mandate on the spot in a group meeting for all to see, revise, and finalize.

In high-functioning groups, committee membership and leadership is a thoughtful and controlled activity. Publicly calling for volunteer leadership or appointing a person to a committee who is not in the room rarely works well. Be thoughtful and strategic about identifying committee chairs and members; select people who understand and believe in the mandate.

In principle, most conflicts are based on misunderstandings. When we make the effort to truly understand the other's perspective and when we have shared understanding of future expectations, conflict often goes away.

Practical Tip: When in conflict, do something about it. Either change your attitude about it so it is no longer a conflict for you or work directly with your adversary. You might try these steps:

1. Pause. Breathe. Step away. Do not immediately react with words or actions you might regret later.

2. Share stories. Tell how the conflict came to be, what it was like from your perspective, and what it is like now. Listen to the other person's story, how it was for them, and how it is now. Try to understand how the other person's experience could lead them to their way of thinking and acting.

3. Share feelings. How does the conflict make you feel? Figure this out and share it. No one can argue with your feelings. Try to understand how others feel.

4. Share underlying interests. Why is this so important to you? What is the need in you that resolving this conflict will satisfy? What are your underlying, long-term interests? Share your answers to these questions and listen to the answers of others.

5. What are you going to do about it? Speak for yourself: what are *you* going to do differently so underlying interests are achieved? Listen to what others intend to do. You might want to write down intentions in the form of a written agreement or contract.

6. Do it. Things will not change if people do not actually *do* things differently. Take responsibility for acting out your new intentions as best you can.

In principle, when there is a core consensus—things that everyone in an organization understands and agrees to—we are more apt to let committees and individuals throughout the organization make decisions by means other than consensus. Managers and workers are trusted to make swift individual and small group decisions on a day-to-day basis because they understand and believe in the organization's core mission and values. When we know we agree on the basics, we trust each other on the details.

Practical tip: Know and shape the core consensus of your group. Make sure you understand your group's mission and values and work to improve them. When staff and committees hold the same values as you, trust their findings and recommendations. Trust individuals and teams throughout the organization to make decisions on your behalf.

When staff and committees hold the same values as you, trust their findings and recommendations.

In principle, when I disagree with someone's particular idea or action it does not mean I have to disagree with them about everything. Using disagreement from one battle as ammunition for another battle works well if you want to perpetuate fighting. If you want to perpetuate peace, it works well to contain disagreement to the particular issue at hand. Peacemakers know how to respectfully disagree about one thing and at the same time work well together on another thing.

Practical Tip: Enter every discussion as a new discussion with a positive outlook and an open mind about your fellows, regardless of past or other present disagreements. Don't hold grudges, seek revenge, or use a person's stance on one issue as a weapon against them on another issue.

Just because I think your idea is wrong or your behavior is inappropriate does not mean I think you are a bad person; it just means that I disagree with that particular idea or behavior, that's all. I am always willing to work with you, with an open mind and a positive attitude, to make the best decisions for our group.

Using disagreement from one battle
as ammunition for another battle
works well if you want to perpetuate fighting.

In principle, members of high-functioning groups are focused on the success of the group as a whole rather than on who should get credit or blame within the group. Harry Truman said, "It is amazing what you can do if you do not care who gets the credit." Similarly, groups get more done when unconcerned with assigning blame.

Rather than spend energy accounting for past individual credit or blame, it is better to invest lessons from the past into future good group decisions. When I believe in my group I know that, over the long run, what is good for the group will be good for me—probably better for me than I could ever have achieved on my own.

Practical Tip: Give your ideas and efforts to the group without conditions, without lingering ownership. Welcome contributions from others without jealousy, without resentment. Show public appreciation for others in your group. Own your share of things gone wrong and credit the group for things gone right.

A mark of a high-functioning team is that each member wants to make other members look good.

In principle, the cause of most criticism is the critic's need to react to something painful, yet public reaction often causes more pain. When you think someone's action or statement deserves criticism, first consider why. Will criticizing make you feel better? Teach them a lesson? You can probably accomplish these by criticizing privately. You might even achieve the first one by talking with a friend, or yelling or crying; get it off your chest. If you want to criticize in order to start a fight or create conflict, then you might want to do it publicly (for instance, send an e-mail to more people than the person you are criticizing). Sometimes that is what is called for, but only sometimes, when more peaceful means of achieving the group mission are exhausted.

Practical Tip: When you have an adverse reaction to someone's words or actions, do not react right away. First try to understand the behavior or words better. Be thoughtful about the reason for your reaction; what purpose will it serve? Only when you think your group needs public conflict should you publicly criticize. Otherwise, talk privately with the person you have an issue with. Start with asking a question about what they said or did.

PS: Another reason we sometimes criticize is to make someone feel small. This is never a good reason for public or private criticism. Good group decisions result when people make each other feel big, valued, appreciated.

Only when you think your group needs public conflict should you publicly criticize.

In principle, when parties cannot agree on an issue the next peaceful step is for them to decide how they are going to decide the issue. For instance, "We can't agree on the floor plan for the new building, so we're going to spend time on this at our next meeting, hear both sides, and vote. Is that okay with everyone?" If everyone can agree on how the thorny issue will be decided, that's progress toward agreement. When we send something to a committee or say something like, "Let's ask Louise and let her decide," we are making a decision about how to decide.

When diplomats or politicians spend time on meeting arrangements, seating plans, and the details of meeting agendas—the conditions under which the parties agree to meet—they are really deciding how they will decide. They are building agreement.

Practical Tip: When it seems like you are stuck and cannot decide something, at least decide how you will decide. Name a next step that moves you in the direction of eventual agreement. Make a plan for a future discussion and vote, send it to a small group or committee with a specific charge, or name a third party decider.

In principle, the center of a circle is equidistant from all points on its perimeter. We need to know the edges to know the center. To know what's centrally acceptable to a group of decision makers, it helps to know the outer limits of acceptability: what's unacceptable.

Practical Tip: Say wild ideas. Make bold proposals. Be provocative. Know that the group is actually well-served when someone responds, "Now that's going too far," or, "That's stepping over the line." Like a flashlight investigating a dark basketball court, shine it all over to find the boundaries.

If you are having a hard time defining how something should be, work for awhile on defining how it should not be. Try stuff on so you know what doesn't fit. Explore side roads so you know which ones dead end. Work inward from what you know is out of bounds.

PS: Don't be attached to clothes that don't fit or roads that go nowhere.

In principle, peace comes through shared understanding, and shared understanding comes through listening. If you hear things incorrectly, or not at all, you're likely to proceed on false assumptions, which are likely to give way later and cause conflict. The best way to ensure good listening is to demonstrate it.

Practical Tip: Are you listening? Prove it. After you have heard someone say something, demonstrate to them that you heard them and understood what they said. Saying "I understand" is not a demonstration.

As you listen, show that you are paying attention with silent expressions and perhaps an encouraging word or two.

After listening, reflect back what you heard. Ideally, repeat the main points, using a mix of their words and some of your own, and try to name their feelings. Like, "My, that must have made you feel angry." Let them judge if you got it right. And if you missed, no problem: try different words and talk it through until you "get it," and they agree that you get it.

The ultimate demonstration: act in ways that prove that you listened and understood.

In principle, it helps to take ownership of what I hear, which may be different from what the speaker intended. Messages often get changed between how they are launched and how they land. The person talking often means one thing yet the person listening often hears it differently. This is due to differences in culture and context. It is nobody's fault.

When I begin a sentence with "I heard," rather than "You said," it acknowledges that I might not have heard it the way you intended. Speaking from my own perspective, using "I messages," is disarming, safe, nonjudgmental, humble.

Practical Tip: Don't tell someone what they said, what they launched. Rather, use your own words to describe what you heard, how the words landed on you. This allows the speaker to clarify any difference between launch and land, which furthers understanding, which contributes to good group decisions.

In principle, how things look depends on where you sit. It's not that one is right and one is wrong, simply that the views are different.

In hierarchical relationships, the person or group at the top has a wider view than the people or groups below. The supervisor considers many things of relative importance at a high level. The subordinate considers fewer things in greater detail. Even though the views may seemingly disagree, each is doing their job, seeing things from their proper perspective.

In other relationships too, our viewpoints are different by design. Tension and initial disagreement are expected. Good group decisions result when we consider all the different views, work out the tension, and identify what's best for the group as a whole.

Practical Tip: Rather than spend energy arguing which view is correct, assume that all views are correct. Use all available perspectives to better understand what you are looking at.

Ask group members to say how it is for them, how things look from where they sit. Ask people outside the group, "What does it look like from out there?" Listen without judgment.

If you are asked to give your view, offer it without expectation that it will prevail. Speak for yourself, from your own perspective. Humbly offer a piece of the puzzle to help create the larger picture.

How things look depends on where you sit.

In principle, the shortest distance between two points is a straight line. When it comes to communications between two people, the shorter the better. It's often easier to get information indirectly, and usually more fun. But indirect information is more like entertainment than fact. Direct communication builds true understanding.

Practical Tip: If you are wondering what someone thinks about something, or why they did something, or what they plan to do in the future, ask them directly. Do not speculate about it with others. Do not proceed based on assumptions. Get the story straight from the source. If you want someone to know what you think, or why you did something, or what you plan to do, tell them. Do not be silent, sneaky, or circuitous and "let them figure it out." When you hear information indirectly like "she thinks this," or "he said that," know that what you are hearing is out of context, altered by the messenger, and only one side of the story.

Good group decisions are built on true understanding and true understanding comes straight from the source.

In principle, moving quickly often seems like a good idea but moving quickly in the wrong direction simply gets you to the wrong place fast. Most groups have a high need for quick achievement. We have all heard someone say, "Enough talk, let's just do something!" And we have all seen groups charge off quickly and with much enthusiasm...in the wrong direction.

Practical Tip: Even when under pressure to accomplish something in a hurry, resist the temptation to achieve a quick, although shabby, result. Quality group decisions, like anything of quality, require upfront investment. Determine your objective before springing into action. Spend some time planning. Read the directions. Check out the map. As Bob Dylan says, "I know my song well before I start singing."[12]

No matter how slowly you go, if you are headed in the right direction you might eventually get there.

In principle, trust grows from the link between what we say and what we do. People trust you less if you do not do what you say you will do. Often the problem is not that you just couldn't get to the thing done that you said you would, it's that you didn't speak truth when you volunteered in the first place. Often the error is not that we didn't *do* something, it's that we *said* we would do something.

Practical Tip: Before you publicly (in a meeting, for instance) volunteer for anything, consider the commitment you are making. For every commitment you make, write something down, either on your calendar or on a to-do list. Don't just say "I'll do this or that" because it sounds good in the moment. Words without action are just words and it is action that builds trust.

Often the error is not that we didn't do something,
it's that we said we would do something.

In principle, each group of decision makers is part of a larger group or larger community. Ultimately, we are all part of the great community we call Earth.

I want what is best for my group, but which group? Over the long run, it is not okay for my local group to profit at the expense of my larger group—that simply shifts expenses to others. Over the long run, doing what is best for my club is not okay if it hurts my town. Doing what is best for my town is not okay if it hurts my country. Doing what is best for my country is not okay if it hurts Earth community.

Practical Tip: As your group makes decisions, consider the impact of those decisions on other groups and over time. Expand the circle of concern all the way to Earth community and into the future. Decide things locally that will help the whole world. Decide things now that will help our kids and our kids' kids. To make good group decisions, we resist the temptation to be guided entirely by local, short-term gain.

It is not okay for my local group
to profit at the expense of my larger group.

In principle, e-mail is an efficient way to communicate in groups, but it is a relatively new way of communicating that we are still getting used to. E-mail is instant, like conversation; enduring, like a written document; and able to be copied and distributed like nothing we have ever known. The combination of these attributes makes it rather like a chainsaw: very effective when used properly, very dangerous when used on impulse or in anger.

E-mail is most effective when used to convey facts quickly. E-mail is most destructive when used to convey a negative reaction to something, like a previous e-mail. It is so quick and easy that we are apt to forget that what we write may be distributed far and wide and long after the feelings behind it have subsided. It is so impersonal that we are apt to underestimate its effect on other people's emotions.

And then there is the problem of interpretation: Very few of us are skilled enough to convey exactly what we mean with written words, or discern exactly what written words were meant to convey. E-mail messages are easily misunderstood and misunderstanding is usually at the root of bad decisions.

Practical Tip: Beware of using e-mail to convey negative emotions, arguments, or sarcasm. Be thoughtful and deliberate about who you send to and about forwarding e-mails. Consider if you should send the message at all. If you don't have something nice to say, don't say it by e-mail.

If you don't fully understand something you read in e-mail, don't fill in the blanks with assumptions. If you don't understand what the sender meant, ask them (perhaps by phone or in-person). E-mail is an easy way to say something *not* to someone's face. That can be efficient and/or hurtful. It cuts both ways.

ENFORCEMENT

In principle, decisions without enforcement grow weak and eventually wither. When rules or policies are not enforced it causes confusion, resentment, and conflict. The word *enforcement* comes from a Latin word meaning *strength*. To enforce decisions is to strengthen them.

Practical Tip: Take preventative measures to ensure that members of your group understand the rules of your group. Honor the rules of your group. If you disagree with the rules: Follow them anyway, leave the group, or work in peaceful ways to change the rules.

When you see someone breaking group rules, try these steps:

1. Discuss with them what you saw. Don't ignore it when you see practice out of sync with policy. Such a conversation may bring to light that they "simply didn't know better," or that they interpret the rule differently, or that a larger issue needs to be addressed. If that doesn't work,

2. Point out the consequences of the violation. "When you do _____, it affects others in the following ways: _____." If that doesn't work,

3. Impose a penalty. Ideal penalties inflict just the right amount of hurt in order to tilt the scales toward compliance.

When rules are legitimately crafted through good group processes, it is okay to enforce them for the good of the group. Actually, it's essential for the good of the group.

In principle, groups work best when a facilitator manages the process. When it is someone's job to look after the group's process, everyone else can focus on substance. When I know that someone is managing the order of speakers, I can pay full attention to what is being said.

When there is no objective facilitator and group members can manipulate the process, it tilts power toward a few, limits creativity, and clogs efficiency. It is typical for Congress, state legislatures, and town governments, for instance, to spend a lot of time debating process issues, agenda setting, committee membership, and rules...often in order to influence a particular outcome.

To maximize efficiency, equality, and creativity, high-functioning groups engage a facilitator who works for the group as a whole, manages the process, and does not try to influence the outcome.

Practical Tip: If you want good group decisions, invest in good group facilitation. Like any kind of professional expertise, group facilitation expertise is learned through study and experience. There is a body of knowledge and a proven set of techniques that can move a group forward by leaps and bounds.

Engaging a facilitation expert, whether a paid outsider or volunteer insider, brings knowledge, skill, and objectivity to your group process and substantially increases your chances of making good group decisions.

There is a body of knowledge and a proven set of techniques that can move a group forward by leaps and bounds.

In principle, when we ask for feedback we increase our chances of making good group decisions. If we don't ask we can't expect people to tell us what's going well and not so well. When we do ask we should be open to all answers. Asking for feedback takes courage but gives enlightenment. It helps us see things in new light, reflected off others.

Practical Tip: Ask how you are doing among those who care about what you do. What's working well? What could be better? What questions or ideas do your stakeholders have? Be thankful for all invited feedback, positive or negative. Be open to how you might use it to make improvements.

Take positive comments to heart and share credit with others. When you receive a negative comment, consider that it's probably not about you. It's more likely about a particular idea, behavior, or situation. And, consider that negative comments are sometimes all about the world of the commentator and not about the topic at hand.

See things in new light, reflected off others.

In principle, different ways of deciding should be applied to different types of decisions.

Deciding how things should be—planning—is well-suited to a flat decision-making structure; that is, where several decision makers are equal and all fully participate. Some call this consensus decision making. As a rule, the longer and wider the reach of the plan, the broader and flatter the planning structure should be.

Deciding how to implement plans—doing—is better suited to hierarchical decision-making structure; that is, roles and responsibilities are stacked upon each other. There is a chain of command and accountability up and down the ladder. As a rule, the more expeditious and short-lived a decision is, the better it is to delegate it to an individual within a hierarchy.

Practical Tip: For each decision, first decide the type of decision: Is it more of a planning-type decision or more of an implementation-type decision? Will it have long-term, broad impact or short-term, local impact? Apply a decision-making method appropriate to the nature of the decision. Every group member need not decide small, implementation details. Long-term planning and high-level policy should not be in the hands of just a powerful few.

The longer and wider the reach of the plan
the broader and flatter the planning structure should be.

In principle, every encounter, every meeting, is an opportunity to start anew. It is good to learn from the past but not be artificially constrained by it.

Just because we have spent a lot of money or effort on something (referred to by economists as *sunk costs*) is not by itself justification for spending more. The proper decision criterion for spending money or effort is how it might affect the future, not how it might change the past. Revenge too may create the illusion of making the past better but in fact only makes the future worse.

We cannot change the past by the decisions we make today, but we can change our feelings about the past by making good decisions for tomorrow.

Practical Tip: Glance back over your shoulder, but not so much that you stumble on what's ahead. Let the past inform the future, but not dominate it.

Experiences from our past are like rocks, best used to pile up and stand upon, see clearly, and step off into the future in any direction—not to be used for building walls.

In principle, to make good group decisions we need to hear all perspectives. We need be able to openly disagree with respect and civility. We need to have the courage to speak what's on our minds and hearts even in the face of opposition. When a group's culture makes it not okay to voice certain views or when participants feel intimidated about sharing, those suppressed viewpoints don't go away; they just fester and turn into conflict later.

Practical Tip: Help create a group culture that encourages open sharing of all points of view. Offer encouragement and support to those who express minority opinions, even if you disagree. Stand tall and speak your own truth, and be genuinely open to considering other truths.

Expressing our differing opinions gives us a chance to understand each other better, talk, and inch toward eventual resolution. When views are suppressed it might appear orderly in the short run, but inches us toward eventual conflict.

Suppressed viewpoints don't go away;
they just fester and turn into conflict later.

In principle, a virtue of most decision-making systems such as Robert's Rules of Order is that for a group to consider an idea, at least two members need to think it worthy of the full group's time. A motion needs a second in order to be considered. Requiring that I get one other person bought into my idea before taking up the full group's time assures that the group cannot be dominated by a single person or an untested idea. Further, requiring at least one collaborator enhances creativity.

Practical Tip: Before you take your idea to the whole group, take it to at least one other person first. Be open to feedback and adaptation. Take your idea to someone who could lend credibility and help you take it to others. If initially rejected, try someone else. When at least one other respected group member believes in your idea then perhaps it is time to take it to the full group. If you cannot get at least one other person to believe in your idea, change it.

Requiring at least one collaborator enhances creativity.

In principle, the chances of making good group decisions are greatly increased if all the participants believe that there is good in everyone. We're more likely to do well if we look for the best in each other. For some, believing that there is good in every person is a moral conviction. For others, seeking and bringing out the best in people is just plain practical.

Practical Tip: Act as if there is good in everyone, even when it's not apparent. Treat every person along your path as if they are special. If you believe in God, act as if there is that of God in every person.

To act this way is to give the benefit of the doubt. It is to assume best intentions. It is to be attentive, respectful, supportive, and encouraging. When we look for the best in people rather than the worst, it makes them want to be with us and work with us. When a group is relentlessly seeking out the best from within each person, people give their best to the group and great things are achieved.

GOOD INFORMATION COMPELS

In principle, there are basically three ways to influence the choices people make:

1. Regulate what people cannot do and punish violations.

2. Offer incentives to encourage certain choices.

3. Provide information that rings so true it compels good choices.

If you believe that, for the most part, people want to do the right thing, the most effective and peaceful method of influencing good decisions is to provide good information so *the right thing* becomes self-evident.

For example, Maine has historically had one of the highest teen smoking rates in the nation. We have made laws against teen smoking and punished violators. We have created incentives against smoking such as high taxes on cigarettes. These have not had satisfactory results. Only recently has the rate dramatically declined and it is because we launched an information campaign that made the detrimental health effects of cigarette smoking clear. We provided truthful information on television and radio. For all those teens who *want to do the right thing*, it's now clear what that is.

Practical Tip: Provide all decision makers with the best possible information about the issue being considered. Good, truthful information is extremely compelling.

Actually, good information is the only thing that is truly compelling and results in sustainable decisions.

In principle, gratitude is all about attitude. Gratitude is a choice we make to see good in ourselves, our situation, and the people around us.

Discontent arises in me when there is a gap between what I have and what I want. When the gap is large I am apt to try and close it by getting what I want. Advertisers know this so they breed discontent. They try to persuade me that what I have is not good enough and if I just had more and better stuff I would be happy. Similarly, I am sometimes seduced into thinking that people around me are not good enough and that if they would just change their behaviors I would be happy.

It's okay to want things to be better, but it's not okay to put down ourselves, our situation, or our group in order to justify selfish behavior. A person lacking gratitude is likely to be a drag on good group decisions.

Sometimes getting what we want leads to happiness, but the surer way to close the gap of discontent is to look with gratitude upon that which we already have.

Practical Tip: Take stock of what you have and see the good in yourself, your situation, and your group. Imagine how things could be worse. Reach out and help someone less fortunate. Say thanks.

Discontent arises in me when there is a gap between what I have and what I want.

In principle, when everybody understands and plays by the same rules the experience is much more likely to be fun and rewarding than if people make up or assume their own rules and not everyone understands the rules. Like playground rules posted on a fence, meeting ground rules encourage us to play safe, have fun, and include everyone. Group decision making is more efficient and achieves better results when we have shared expectations of each other.

Practical Tip: Establish meeting ground rules at the start of every meeting—a simple list of ten or fewer statements about how we all agree to behave in the meeting. The group might make a list from scratch or discuss and revise a list proposed by a facilitator or other leader. Many groups use the same set of ground rules meeting after meeting.

All participants should be watchful for compliance with the ground rules and politely point out violations. Review the ground rules regularly and don't hesitate to make additions or changes. Make sure new people understand the ground rules.

*Like playground rules posted on a fence,
meeting ground rules encourage us to
play safe, have fun, and include everyone.*

In principle, high-functioning leadership groups are "hands on" regarding the tasks they are supposed to do and the decisions they are supposed to make. They also understand what tasks and decisions they should keep their hands off. High-functioning leaders delegate responsibility to committees or individuals and then stand aside to let them do their job in their own way with their own creative spirit.

Practical Tip: Before your group takes up an issue, ask "Should we be handling this?" Don't spend unnecessary time on things you have already decided to let others handle. When you give responsibility to others, it helps when the expectations are written and clearly understood.

Good leaders facilitate rather than micro-manage. A mark of a good leader is that their followers become good leaders. Facilitative leaders clarify expectations, offer encouragement, demonstrate exemplary behavior, and let go.

A mark of a good leader is that their followers become good leaders.

In principle, we each have our gifts. Some people are better at some things than others and we all have our good days and bad days. I know of a basketball coach who encourages his team to shoot around before every game and figure out who has the "hot hand," who seems to be particularly gifted that day. Get the ball into the hands of that person, he encourages.

Practical Tip: For any given task on any given day, figure out who is most suited to lead. It could be anyone. If you are not the most able or not top-performing for whatever reasons, support someone who is.

Members of high-functioning groups are flexible and give the ball to whoever is most likely to succeed in the moment, regardless of prior established titles, positions, or plans.

In principle, groups make their best decisions when no single person knows what's best for the group. "No one in this room is smarter than all of us," is a popular phrase among some groups.

When I go into a meeting already sure of what the outcome should be, I am apt to focus on getting my way rather than on what's best for the group as a whole. Knowing in advance how things should be closes off the potential of things being better than I can imagine.

Practical Tip: At the start of every meeting, say to yourself: "I don't know what's best for the group." Begin with an open mind and remain open-minded as long as possible. Maximize the value of your contributions by giving up ownership of them. Release the need to take credit and the need to be a victim. Simply play your right-sized part as best you can and watch the group's best unfold.

Maximize the value of your contributions
by giving up ownership of them.

In principle, an important decision that every group makes is to select its leaders. High-functioning groups give their leaders a little push at the start of their term, special encouragement, a show of confidence. The word *inauguration* evokes the word *augment*: to enhance, increase, make greater.

Practical Tip: When people take on leadership roles in your group, inaugurate them. It need not be a fancy ceremony, but simple words, actions and attitudes that convey: we support you and we trust that you will do your best on our behalf.

Even if you did not agree with their selection, as long as the selection process was honorable, give group leaders the benefit of the doubt from the start. Sometimes people in new leadership roles surprise us with new leadership abilities. When we set new leaders up for success rather than for failure, our groups are more likely to succeed.

In principle, the best things are always built in tiny stages. Often there is the illusion of dramatic change, but even seemingly miraculous changes result from thousands of small steps. Taking small steps forward on a project lets us learn as we go and adjust. Big steps are risky. Small steps are sure-footed. Nature builds in very small increments and achieves very great things.

Practical Tip: Do things small before you do them big, on small stages before big stages. Make use of pilot projects, test cases, and trial runs. Make commitments incrementally. Proceed with many small steps rather than a few giant leaps. When your group wants to rush ahead asking, "What's the biggest step we can take to achieve our objective?" ask also, "What's the smallest step we can take?"

It is better to take a small step in what we know is the right direction than to take a large step in what might be the wrong direction.

Nature builds in very small increments
and achieves very great things.

In principle, a key to achieving big things is to not be distracted by small things. It is good to be passionate about one or two things and it is okay to be indifferent to everything else.

Indifference is simply the absence of feeling for or against. It is to say, "I'm simply not thinking about that right now. I have no judgment about it, good or bad." Having to make judgments about many things waters down our focus and lessens our ability to make good decisions about the most important things.

Practical Tip: Decide what is really important and focus on that. Give yourself and your group freedom to be indifferent toward things currently out of focus. Better to make no judgment than wrong judgment. Better to make good decisions about a few things than bad decisions about a lot of things. It's okay to say, "I don't know what I think about that."

Better to make no judgment than wrong judgment.

In principle, when someone comes into a meeting or a negotiation with an already established position, it limits prospects for creative, innovative, win-win solutions. When I state my position on an issue early in the discussion, my focus thereafter becomes defending my position and trying to persuade others to agree with it. I might even get side-tracked into defending my pride rather than considering what's best for the group.

On the other hand, if I'm able to speak clearly about my interests (what I would like to get out of the issue without attachment to a particular way of getting it) and I'm able to listen openly to others' interests, we have a much better chance of all getting what we want.

Practical Tip: Focus first on what you really want rather than how to get it. If you are leaning toward a particular solution, peel back a layer, dig a bit deeper, and ask, "What desire in me does this solution attempt to satisfy?" Ask yourself, "What is my fundamental interest here?" Identify what you are really interested in, give it words, and speak the words to others. Listen carefully to their words about their interests. As a group, hear and understand all interests before crafting solutions.

Positions spoken early invite argument. Interests spoken early invite win-win, creative solutions.

Focus first on what you really want
rather than how to get it.

In principle, when we decide more than we have to, say more than we have to, or do more than just enough to get the job done, it might cause trouble.

We don't have to decide everything right now. It works well to decide only what we have to, see how that plays out and then decide the next steps. One step at a time.

We don't have to say everything we're thinking. It works to first consider the purpose of speaking and then say just enough to achieve the purpose.

We don't have to do too much, over-fix things, or fix things that aren't really broken. That often causes inefficiency.

Practical Tip: You don't have to do it all right now, or say it all, or decide it all. It's okay to put some decisions off. Break projects into pieces and make decisions in pieces. The smaller the pieces, the less chance of bad decisions with big impact and the more chance of building on lessons learned.

We don't have to decide everything right now.

In principle, it's better to be kind than to be right. The ego in me wants me to be right. The peace seeker in me wants me to be kind. The word *kind* is related to the word *kin*, meaning *family.* To be kind is to treat people like family, as if we were intimately connected over time.

Practical Tip: To contribute to good group decisions I feed the peace seeker within, keep the ego in check, and strive for kindness. I am more interested in my healthy relations with fellow decision makers over the long run than I am in getting my way in the short run. I give unconditionally without expectation of return, free of strings. True kindness is not only free, it's priceless.

In principle, members of high-functioning groups know their roles and play them well. When group members are unsure of their roles they are hesitant to take initiative for fear of embarrassment or offending others. When group decision making is inefficient it is often because roles are not well defined and/or group members are not playing their parts.

Lines are limits, a word derived from Latin *limes*. Lines are boundaries and it is helpful to know them and work within them. A line is also a set of words delivered in a play. In any good production, each player knows their lines.

Practical Tip: Take time to define expectations of each role within your group and make sure the expectations are widely understood. This is more than defining jobs, it is defining decision-making steps and expecting each member to keep step with the process; not act out of order. It is knowing when to weigh in and when to stand aside. It is the wisdom to know the difference between what to accept and what to change.

LEADERSHIP

In principle, leadership is not reserved for only a few and it need not come only from the person at the front of the room. Leadership can be learned and it can come from anywhere. Any member of a group may practice leadership and when leadership comes from many places, outstanding decisions get made and extraordinary things get done.

In a book called *The Leadership Challenge*, Jim Kouzes and Barry Posner report their survey findings about what the world's best leaders do to get extraordinary things done—five fundamental leadership practices: challenge the process, inspire a shared vision, enable others to act, model the way, and encourage the heart.[13]

Practical Tip: Learn about leadership and practice it from wherever you are. It's not about speaking the loudest or appearing the strongest or being in front. It's about developing and sharing vision. It's about being a good example, even in small ways. It's about encouraging others, perhaps behind the scenes. It's asking questions and trying new ways of doing things. It's nurturing passion in others and in ourselves.

You don't have to be a designated leader to practice leadership.

LET THINGS DIE

In principle, groups can spend a lot of time and energy keeping ideas and projects artificially alive. We are all familiar with the agenda item that keeps coming up over and over again but that no one seems to have energy for; or the committee for which energy is fading, attendance is waning, and discussion becomes mostly about process rather than substance. Putting energy into dying things distracts attention from helping other things grow.

That things die is okay. The wonderful thing about dying is that it leads to new life. When things die, the energy goes to other places. Letting things die fertilizes new creativity.

Practical Tip: Make deliberate decisions about what you want to help grow and what you want to let die. Chasing instincts to save everything is inefficient. If a committee or project of your group is dying and it is not something that you care about or have optimism around, don't put energy into keeping it alive.

Plan for dying. Create committees with sunset provisions that require them to die automatically if no one moves to save them, rather than that they live automatically if no one moves to kill them.

When dying things bring sadness, that's okay too. Work to turn those emotions into new resolve for growth and creation of new things.

Chasing instincts to save everything is inefficient.

In principle, just because a person is talking doesn't necessarily mean they are contributing, or that they are the only one contributing. Most of the time in a group decision setting, listening is the best contribution we can make. It is through listening, not talking, that we develop understanding, compassion, and creative solutions.

Practical Tip: Bite your tongue, hold your horses, cool your jets. To listen, don't talk. Don't be distracted by planning your talk.

If I let you talk first while I listen, it gives me some practical advantages:

1. To hear where you are coming from helps me choose my words. You have likely provided me some new information that I can incorporate.

2. Once you've got your words out you are more likely to be open to hearing mine.

3. Not talking first gives me time to listen within, listen to my own thoughts and feelings.

I help the group's decision process when I consider my inner thoughts, how I really feel about something, so that when my words are spoken they are aligned with inner truth.

LOOSE IN THE HARNESS

In principle, they say a horse runs best when loose in the harness. It helps if someone has the reins. It helps to have a good communication link between the driver and the horse, a way to send messages. It helps that the horse has boundaries, not unbridled freedom. Yet within the harness the horse runs free.

Groups work best when loose within structure. A group's harness is made of ground rules, the agenda, and maybe a facilitator, chair, or coach.

Practical Tip: As the group leader or facilitator, be firm about the decision making or meeting structure. Send clear messages to guide behavior. Yet within the discipline that you establish, encourage your team to go wild. Give your group some slack. Giddy-up.

Within the harness the horse runs free.

In principle, more important than winning any particular decision is the health of the relationships that we carry into the next decision. Is it worth it to jeopardize a long-term relationship in order to win a short-term decision? Maybe, but not likely.

Further, a group member holding out for a win may block the group's forward progress and perpetuate conflict. They are sure that they are right and that the group is wrong. Is an individual win more important than group peace? Sometimes, but not often.

The good thing about losing is that it often allows one to move on, let go of the battle. Compared to being stuck in conflict, losing and moving on can be very beneficial.

Practical Tip: Be thoughtful about when to fight and when to accept. Stand tall enough to see beyond the immediate conflict. Is it more important that *I* win now or that *we* win over the long run?

*The good thing about losing
is that it often allows one to move on.*

LOVE

In principle, it is love that truly changes hearts and transforms people, not power or rules. It is love that compels sustained changes in behavior, not oaths or doctrines. It is love that provides a willingness to give and it is love that helps us accept, let go, and find peace.

Most group decision-making models encourage that we not include love in the mix. We're supposed to be objective, rational, unemotional. This works well on the field of battle where the goal is to beat the other guys. But it doesn't work well when we are trying to find win-win solutions, peaceful solutions. Peace asks us to love our neighbors.

Practical Tip: It's okay to allow love into your group decision making. This means encouraging passion...and compassion. It means treating everyone as a valued contributor, and no one as an enemy. It means making decisions not just with your head, but also with your heart. It means paying attention not only to the best available knowledge, but to wisdom.

I once heard someone say that "Wisdom equals knowledge plus love."

In principle, to manage any activity—to know what to do more of, less of, and what to do differently—we need to be able to measure it. We ask, "How is it going?" And to measure any activity we need a measuring stick, something against which to compare.

Some call it "benchmarking," where progress is compared to:

1. A reference group of similar activities or organizations (like an average or median),

2. One's own past performance (like how you did last year, or over the past several years), or,

3. A quantifiable goal (like a fundraising thermometer/sign posted in front of the building).

Without anything to compare against, we cannot actually say anything about the success of an activity or how to manage it for greater success.

Practical Tip: When your group decides on a new activity or policy, decide also how you will know if it is successful. Set a goal. Be specific. Write it in such a way that you will be able to know if you achieved it. If possible, state the goal relative to the performance of other similar groups or activities, or relative to your own group's past performance.

Measuring progress not only helps you manage future activities, it encourages better performance.

In principle, we all make mistakes. It is part of being human. Mistakes are often painful in the short term but useful in the long term. Mistakes teach us how to do things better, how to make better decisions.

It's often unfair to judge a person just because they made a mistake. The better basis for judgment is how one handles one's mistake.

We are most useful to our groups when we acknowledge our mistakes, try to make things right, and maintain self worth.

Practical Tip: Turn mistakes into opportunities to demonstrate your good character. Admit your mistake, apologize, try to fix it, take stock of lessons learned, and move on.

Do not let mistakes bring you down but rather make you strong. Do not judge against someone who makes an honest mistake and handles it with integrity.

Graduate from small mistakes to higher stakes.

In principle, there is something to be said for a moral compass handed down to us from our ancestors. As food customs protect us from poisoning, moral customs prevent bad things from happening.

Basic moral themes shared across cultures and continents are trustworthy guides: themes such as respect and compassion for all people, honesty, fairness, self worth, and respect for nature. Groups that consider universal morality when making decisions are more likely to make decisions that head us in good directions.

Practical Tip: Even if you are not breaking a law, or perhaps not getting caught, if you are breaking a widely shared moral code then there is a good chance that bad things will result.

When trying to decide the right thing to do, remember your moral compass...worth following when otherwise off the charts.

In principle, if group members have not agreed to a particular morality or set of values, it is not okay to expect or impose that particular morality or set of values. People become uncomfortable when it feels like a specific moral code is being imposed without permission. Imposing morality creates enemies.

On the other hand, if your group has a moral code it is right to honor it. Speaking a certain morality without acting on it also creates enemies.

Practical Tip: Do not impose unwelcome morality. Act out agreed morality. Work to change group morality using agreed group processes.

For example, if a neighborhood association's stated purpose and other governing documents say nothing of environmental values, group members should not impose environmental values as if they were group values. It is not okay to suggest that someone is being "anti-group" if they are being "anti-environment." If you would like environmental values to become group values then work for that within the rules. Request discussion about it. Make a proposal. Practice environmental values in your own yard and in all ways that are not contrary to group decisions. But in the absence of stated group morality, it is not okay to behave as if such morality is shared by the group as a whole.

In principle, you know when a dog is happy to see you, and when not. People wag and bark too, in different ways. When two dogs approach each other wagging, expecting friendship, the outcome is almost always good. When one or more dogs are barking, it is hard to make good group decisions.

Practical Tip: Approach people wagging, expecting good things. Carry a sunny disposition. Look for the good in every person and in every situation...and let your optimism show. Wag more. Bark less.

In principle, one vote per person works well to assess support for a single issue or to choose a single candidate, but to establish several top priorities from among a long list or to assess group preferences among multiple choices, try a multi-vote.

A multi-vote is where each group member is given three or more votes to allocate among several alternatives. For instance, after identifying several ways to solve a problem and writing them all on the wall, each group member might be given three small sticker-dots (votes) and told, "Put your sticker-dots on your three favorite ideas." Placing two or even three stickers on a single item is typically allowed. After voting, the whole group can step back and see how the votes are distributed among all the ideas. There is an immediate shared sense of the group's top priorities.

Practical Tip: Use a multi-vote to decide where to focus conversation. Rather than continue conversation about a whole list of ideas, multi-vote results indicate which ideas are worth further group consideration, and which are not.

To use multi-vote results to actually make decisions, have repeated rounds of multi-voting with each round limited to the top priorities of the previous round.

Apart from using sticker-dots, there are several other multi-vote methods such as hand-written or on-line surveys. Some groups use keypad voting where each participant is given a remote keypad and results are digitally tabulated by a computer and displayed graphically on a screen.

Multi-voting is a great way to quickly engage all participants and immediately see preferences of the group as a whole.

MY FIRST THOUGHT IS PROBABLY NOT MY BEST

In principle, my initial reaction—my first thought—is very rarely my best thought. Often my first thought is absurd and shows me how *not* to react.

Like first brush strokes on a canvas, first thoughts provide a starting place for more refined thoughts, for subsequent brush strokes. First thoughts, like initial brush strokes, are rarely worth sharing. In fact, sharing first thoughts can be deeply counter-productive to good group decisions.

Practical Tip: Just because I think something, doesn't mean I have to say it or act on it. When we share first thoughts we run a substantial risk of offending others, saying things we will regret, and requiring the group to spend time on issues that turn out to be a waste of time. Best to sit with our thoughts until a clear picture emerges of what we want to say.

Just because I think something,
doesn't mean I have to say it or act on it.

In principle, there are at least two pieces to every puzzle, at least two parts to every solution. No solution to a problem is entirely in the hands of just one person.

For example, people at the back of a room might have a hard time hearing the speaker at the front. When this happens someone is apt to suggest to the speaker: "Speak up." But another solution is in the hands of the listeners: "Move closer."

If I have a problem with someone's behavior, one solution is for them to change. Another solution is for me to change. I can change how I interact with them or I can change my attitude toward them.

When I assume my problem is entirely because of someone else, I am hiding an important part of the solution. When I deny my part, I am in the way of the group moving forward.

We can spend a lot of time and energy wishing our group was different, complaining about our group, questioning other group members about their ways. But there is only one question that leads to real change: "What am I going to do about it?"

Practical Tip: With every problem remember that there are multiple parts to the solution. Ask, "What's my part?" If you want the problem solved, act in ways that will help solve the problem rather than talk about how *others* should solve it.

Be the change that you want for your group, for your world.

***No solution to a problem
is entirely in the hands of just one person.***

In principle, whenever a group identifies something that needs to be done, it helps to name a "lead;" that is, the person responsible for taking the next step.

If a new committee is formed, who is responsible for convening the first meeting? If we need more information about something, who will actually gather it and report back to the group? Things that no one is directly responsible for tend to get dropped. Naming a "go to" person (lead) for each thing lets everyone know who to call if they have a question about it.

Being named lead on something gives me a sense of responsibility and compels me to do a good job.

Practical Tip: Before adjourning a meeting, make sure that a name is attached to every action item. Encourage people to take leads. If you believe something is important, consider taking the lead yourself.

Don't assign the lead to someone not present without their permission. If an item arises that no one is willing to take the lead on, let it drop. This is a clear sign that there is not enough energy among the group to actually implement the thing even though it "seems like a good idea."

Groups are terrific at generating ideas, but individual leadership gets things done.

NO COMPLAINING WITHOUT CONTRIBUTION

In principle, if I haven't tried to make something better or if I'm not willing to help make it better, I have no business complaining about it. Rather than stand outside the circle and complain about the decisions others make, I do well to appreciate those who are willing to do the hard work of group decision making.

In fact, complaining without contribution actually hurts group decision making because it demoralizes current decision makers and discourages potential new ones.

Practical Tip: If I am unhappy or disappointed with the decisions of my group (perhaps an organization I belong to or perhaps my government), before criticizing I should first be grateful for the decision makers' efforts.

Second, I try to understand their perspective, how it's different from mine, and why.

Third, if my discontent is real and lasting, I ask myself, "What am I willing to do about it?" I ask myself, "Am I willing to change my personal behavior in some way to make things better? Am I willing to somehow participate in the next round of decision making?"

A thoughtful statement about what you are going to do—followed up with action—is always much more effective than a lazy statement about what someone else should do.

In principle, the next great idea might come from anywhere, not just from the person with the most power or who talks the most. Groups seeking truly creative decisions invite and make room for creative suggestions from all participants. When naturally dominant people are humble and when naturally shy people are courageous, prospects for good group decisions are dramatically increased.

Practical Tip: If you have a strong opinion about something or recognize that you are dominating, consider even for a second that there might be a better way than yours; there might be better ideas out there worth hearing. The less you talk, the more you hear.

If you are part of a group where someone is dominating the conversation, speak up and say that you would like to hear from others. Say, "We appreciate your views but would like to hear other views also. Is there someone else who would like to weigh in on this?" In this way it's not about shutting someone up, rather it's about wanting to hear from others.

Appreciate and validate the dominant comments, then move on.

Consider even for a second
that there might be a better way than yours.

In principle, money absolutely matters but it's not the only thing that matters. Money represents many valuable things yet fails to account for many things we value. Group decisions all about money often fail to consider adverse long-term effects on our emotions, on our relations, and on other groups, including future generations. This results in conflict at other times or in other places.

Money-based decisions also tend to miss opportunities that do not show up in the financial accounts of the alternatives: opportunities to increase long-term trust, peace, happiness, and other rewards in waiting.

Decisions motivated by profit tend to focus on short-term selfish impact rather than long-term community impact.

Practical Tip: When making group decisions, consider *all* potential costs and benefits. Consider how it will affect long-term peace among the group. Consider impacts outside the scope of your financial accounting: impacts on society at large, on the environment, on future generations.

The golden rule is: "Treat others as you would like to be treated," not, "He with the most gold rules." Actually, happiness does not result from having money or from ruling other people; it results from being at peace.

In principle, we each have a personality type, hardwired into us, not likely to change. There are many methods of assessing personality types, Myers-Briggs the most popular among them. Most assessments consist of a written test that reveals one's basic type. Categorizing people into basic types has been going on since 400 B.C. Hippocrates called them the four temperaments. In medieval times they were called the four humors.

With a certain personality type come certain personality traits. Our type has to do with how we learn, how we act, how we perceive others and the world, and how some abilities come naturally to us and some don't.

Practical Tip: To help make good group decisions, I keep in mind that people are different, not everyone is good at everything, and that others see things differently than me, instinctively. When someone doesn't do something the way I would do it, I figure it's not his intention to be difficult, he's just different.

That people are different from me is never their fault. Actually, it's their gift. I try to embrace and build on the gifts of others, and my own.

> *That people are different from me*
> *is never their fault.*

In principle, an amateur may follow the script perfectly but a professional knows when to change the script or even leave it entirely, depending on the energy of the audience. A novice may know the rules but a veteran knows the exceptions. It is good to have scripts, plans, and rules, but experience warns against unwavering allegiance to them.

Practical Tip: Keep in mind that plans and rules are never an end in themselves but are rather just means to an end. Plans and rules are there to keep us on track toward long-term goals, but if we get off track we need to change plans and rules accordingly.

If a meeting agenda is not achieving the meeting objectives, change it. If an annual work plan is not resulting in the right amount or quality of work getting done, change it. If a law is not having the desired effect, change it.

If you find that a plan or rule is not working for your group, don't make an independent decision to ignore it. Rather, work within established group processes to change it.

Achieving long-term ends requires ever-changing means.

> *A novice may know the rules*
> *but a veteran knows the exceptions.*

In principle, leaders are often criticized for changing their minds on issues because it apparently indicates weakness, inconsistency, lack of commitment to a particular doctrine. It may indicate that one is subject to influence. Yet groups make their best decisions when every group member is subject to influence, when each one of us is open to hearing and acting on the wisdom of others and on new information.

Changing one's mind for trivial or self-serving reasons may indicate weakness, but changing one's mind in the face of new truths indicates growth and evolution.

Practical Tip: Know your values and morals but do not be so attached to them that they cause you to deny new truths. Be in touch with your beliefs but also open to new information and new beliefs. One of the most powerful and helpful things one can say in a meeting is, "Well, okay, I've changed my mind."

The thing we can count on about our world is that it is always changing. To make good group decisions we need to be open to changing with it.

Know your values and morals,
but do not be so attached to them
that they cause you to deny new truths.

In principle, speaking on behalf of others is fraught with potential conflict. It warrants caution. It encourages assumptions and blurs understanding. It slows and can even clog the decision-making process. To avoid misunderstanding, conflict, and inefficiency, it helps to ask questions of each other in real-time conversation. The most efficient and best decisions are usually made face-to-face among those most affected by the decision.

Sometimes people speak on behalf of others to stir up trouble or for entertainment, and it often amounts to exactly that.

Practical Tip: Resist the temptation to speak on behalf of others. Speak for yourself and encourage others to speak for themselves. Help create a group culture of support and respect so that people are not shy about speaking and standing up for themselves.

When information is delivered on be*half* of others take it for what it is: once removed, *half* the story. Not to be ignored perhaps, but not to base a decision on.

There are times when speaking on behalf of someone else or a class of people is appropriate, in fact called for. There are times that a group should rightfully consider voices not present. However, a position on behalf of someone not present is rarely cause to block a decision. When forward progress is halted on behalf of someone not present, conflict erupts and inefficiencies abound.

When information is delivered on behalf of others
take it for what it is:
once removed, half the story.

In principle, there are many things out of my control but, for most of us, within my control is how I spend my time and money. I get to decide what to participate in and what to opt out of. I cannot control a television show but I can opt out of watching it. I cannot control how a consumer product is made but I can opt out of buying it.

Another choice I have when I confront something I do not like is to try to defeat it. This is doing battle, sometimes in a straight path of destruction. Opting out is a winding path.

Both fighting and opting out affect the provider of the product or message we dislike. When people in large numbers opt out of buying a product, the provider stops providing it. Boycotting is a very effective way to make good group decisions, and peaceful.

Practical Tip: Don't opt out of agreements already made but with new choices, steer your time and money away from things you oppose. Each personal choice you make sends a message.

As a group, make choices based on participation. If people aren't showing up or otherwise contributing to a particular activity, discontinue it.

Steer your time and money
away from things you oppose.

ORIENTATION

In principle, orienting new people to your group prevents conflict and improves creativity. When new people come in without a solid understanding of the group's purpose and how things are done, there will be mismatched expectations and then conflict. Good orientation ensures we are all on the same page headed in the same direction.

Orientation can foster a sense of belonging and provide structure for creative contributions. Alternatively, it can reveal a lack of fit and indicate "let's not go through with it." Both outcomes are valuable.

Practical Tip: Be deliberate about orienting new members. Do not assume that a new member knows what the group is about, how things are done, and what is planned for the future. Provide each new member with information about the group's purpose, strategic direction, and expectations for member behavior. Someone should spend one-on-one time with every new member.

Provide honest answers to questions even if it might turn someone away.

Be clear about where the group is headed and sincere about the invitation to come along.

In principle, if we want things to be different we have to see or do things differently. If a group of people are seemingly unable to solve a problem among themselves, perhaps they don't have the wherewithal among themselves. If a group seems stuck in its ways— unenthusiastic, mediocre—perhaps it's time for some outside influence.

Outside influences can jar things loose, knock things off track, light motivational fires; exactly what might be needed.

Practical Tip: Always bring new influences into your group: outside speakers, visitors, new information. Seek out those with special expertise and relevant experiences. Do not be threatened by outside influences; welcome them.

Outside influences can help you confirm that you are on the right track or inspire you towards a new track. Both are good.

*If we want things to be different
we have to see or do things differently.*

In principle, if a disagreement is caused by an outside issue that has nothing to do with the group issue at hand, then it must be dealt with outside the group.

An outside issue is a disagreement because of, for example, some incident between the parties that happened years ago and was never dealt with, or because of a mental disorder or perhaps an addiction. Or perhaps the conflict is related to a misconception closely-held since childhood or an illogical fear.

Outside issues are usually personal and often completely unrelated to the group's immediate business, although they can get hugely in the way of the group's immediate business. Outside issues prevent people from seeing or acting clearly.

If an outside issue is in the way, agreement will only come about if the issue is dealt with. If an outside issue is not dealt with and disagreeing parties are unable to let go of the issue, then the group is at risk of being paralyzed, held hostage by an issue that they have no ability to fix.

Practical Tip: Once you recognize that an outside issue is the cause of a disagreement, encourage the parties to deal with it outside the group. Perhaps mediation is called for, perhaps therapy.

If those with outside issues are unwilling or unable to get outside help, take a vote, bring in an arbitrator, or somehow otherwise resolve the issue—even over objections. Someone might lose but losing is not always bad. Sometimes it's the only thing that will allow some people to move forward.

It is better that one or two people lose a single issue than for the group as a whole to get bogged down and unable to make progress.

In principle, the three fundamental steps that help make a meeting great are:

1. Plan what you are going to meet about,

2. Actually meet according to the plan, and,

3. Write up the meeting results.

Practical tip: Prior to an upcoming meeting, the meeting facilitator (or whoever is going to run the meeting) and group leaders should huddle and get clear on the meeting objectives, agenda, roles, how it will be recorded, and logistics such as advance notices, space, food, nametags, etc. Talk it through and plan out how each part of the meeting will work. Advance planning increases chances that you will have on hand the things you need for the meeting to go well, and sharing the plan in advance increases chances that participants will come prepared and that their expectations will be on target.

Then, run the meeting according to plan, although always prepared to be flexible and responsive to things unplanned. Meeting according to plan provides security for participants.

After, provide participants with a writeup that is more than a simple, chronological transcript. Organize the thoughts and stories shared, name the themes discussed, and format the writeup so it is pleasant to read and easy to refer to later. In the writeup you can provide a logical organizational structure even if things seemed quite confusing during the actual meeting.

Don't skimp on the pre-planning or the post-writeup. These are the two things that often distinguish a great meeting from a mediocre meeting.

In principle, group decisions are creations and often benefit from *re*creation. When the group gets stuck it helps to take a break, call a recess, change perspective, and then come at it again. Engage in recreation.

Fun is often underrated in group decision making. Who says you can't have fun while making good group decisions? I say that having fun helps make better decisions.

Practical Tip: Work hard together, play hard together. Get to know each other off topic and off site. Do fun, physical activities. Even on topic and on site, build in breaks and games to shake up the focus and encourage creativity.

When your creation seems stalled, try recreation.

In principle, it's rarely beneficial to say the first thing that comes to mind. I do not have to say the first thing I think. Even when there's a sense of urgency—especially when there's a sense of urgency—I'm better off if I take time to breathe, reflect, and consider my words before speaking them.

A reflective pause helps me avoid saying something that I will later regret. When I say regretful things it causes unnecessary tension and potentially huge inefficiencies in my group.

Practical Tip: In a group setting, honor a moment of silence before and after each comment, like bookends. If tensions in a group are dangerously high, call for a break or a few moments of silence before proceeding. As a group participant, refrain from hasty reactions.

We have heard, "Don't just sit there, do something!" There is a healthy alternative: "Don't just do something, sit!"

Thank God I have learned the value of placing a pause between receiving and reacting. I have seen how the peacefulness of one breath can avert a windstorm of trouble.

Thank God I have learned the value
of placing a pause
between receiving and reacting.

RESENTMENTS HAVE ROOTS IN EXPECTATIONS

In principle, when we have expectations of others that don't pan out it often leads to resentment which often brews discontent which often causes conflict. I have heard someone say that expectations are planned resentments.

The surest way to avoid resentment is to not have expectations. When I fall into a victim role it's helpful to remember that I am rarely a victim of others and often I am a victim of my own expectations.

Practical Tip: As a participant in group decisions, I try hard not to develop false expectations. I expect from people *only* that they have specifically agreed to, and even then I keep in mind that most people are not capable of doing all that they agree to.

I focus on the good things that my group and the people in it have done, and what they could do, rather than what they should do according to my expectations.

Expectations are planned resentments.

REVENGE IS NEVER A REASON

In principle, just because you did something bad to me is never a reason for me to do something bad to you. Doing something for revenge or to *get even* just makes more bad things happen.

Sometimes we justify harming someone to *teach them a lesson*. If this is my goal, I should first ask, "What is the very best way for the lesson to be taught? Am I the best teacher? Is this the best method?" Probably not.

Another justification is that *harming you will bring me peace.* Really? If it is emotional peace that I want, I should first consider all the possible ways to get it, including changing my own attitudes and behaviors. Among all the options, revenge is rarely the most effective path to personal peace.

Practical Tip: Make decisions always in the best interests of the group going forward. Base decisions only on what you think will make the future better, not on what you think will fix the past. Decide to harm only as a last resort, when there are no other ways to achieve the group's primary interests.

Base decisions only on what you think
will make the future better,
not on what you think will fix the past.

In principle, it is best to make the rules before taking the field, before starting the meeting. When we decide *how* we are going to make decisions before we find ourselves in the tension of making them, it lowers our chances of conflict. It is much easier to establish proposal-development steps and decision criteria in the hypothetical rather then when actually confronted with a real proposal and with real personalities.

"We'll figure out the rules as we go," rarely turns out fair and often leads to conflict and resentment.

Establishing rules of engagement beforehand lets everyone know what to expect, gives everyone equal opportunity to participate, and increases chances of creative, peaceful decisions.

Practical Tip: Before you get to the hard decisions, first establish who gets to vote and who does not, how proposals get developed and discussed, and norms of behavior for meetings. For many groups, such rules are embodied in bylaws and meeting ground rules. Imagine the tough situations before they arrive and decide in advance how they will be handled.

Establishing and enforcing rules does not limit creativity, but rather encourages it. Knowing what to expect gives us courage to fully participate.

In principle, values are those things most important to us, the things we value. For most people, they are ideals, beliefs, rules to live by. We are generally drawn to people who share our values. At the core of every defined group of people are shared values.

Practical Tip: Discuss values as a group and make a written, short, agreed-to list of the values you have in common. Simply having a discussion about values helps us understand each other. Deciding which values we share defines our group and helps people decide if they want to join the group and it also helps people decide to leave. A written list of shared values also serves as a *code of ethics*, a place to turn for guidance when the decision making gets tough.

Shared values are the steadfast ground on which we stand when things are in turmoil.

SHARED VISION REQUIRED

In principle, it is a shared vision that holds a group together, a common view of how people want things to be different in the future. If my opinion of how things should change doesn't overlap with yours in at least a tiny way, we have no reason to work together.

It may be that we disagree on specific approaches—how much money to spend, who to hire, when to do what—but for a good group decision to result we must have a shared vision of the outcome, where we're heading.

Practical Tip: Identify and write down what we agree that we hope to achieve. For an established group this might be a mission statement, or a vision statement, or a set of goals. For a one-time group (perhaps gathered at a public hearing, for instance), begin with a statement of why the group is gathered and make sure at the outset that everyone is there for the same purpose.

When we may be inclined to disagree, it helps to know we have the same vision.

In principle, nothing breeds success like success. Achieving few or small goals provides motivation for achieving more and bigger goals. When there is a gap between a goal and achieving it, one way to close the gap is to improve ability but another way is to make the goal smaller.

"What do you say to the team?" I asked the coach of young hockey players about to lose their seventh game in a row. "You give them small goals," he replied, "Things they can achieve other than winning the game. Things like more shots on goal or more successful passes than in the last game."

Practical Tip: When it looks like your group is underachieving, when morale is down, establish achievable goals and get some successes under your belt. No matter how small the victory, see what it feels like to win.

Sometimes it is okay to move the bar down. Get over it. Boost morale. Move the bar back up later.

SPEAK YOUR TRUTH AND LET GO

In principle, an extremely valuable contribution I can make to a group decision is to discern my own *truth* and share it with the group. Deep inside, what do I really feel? This requires me to cut through the clutter of all that's on my mind. Discerning my truth requires me to be in touch with my feelings, to be honest with myself.

Sharing my truth requires courage. It might make me feel vulnerable. It might unleash other truths.

Protecting myself requires that I speak my truth and let go of the outcome. How others react to my truth is not my responsibility. Detachment is the secret to peace.

Practical Tip: Speak what's on your heart rather than what's on your mind. Don't get mired in calculating the consequences. Speak your truth and let go of the outcome. One way to be sure you are speaking truth: say only what you feel. No one can argue with what you feel.

Once I was in a meeting and spoke my truth. Afterwards, I became terribly afraid of the consequences. I asked someone, "Did I say the right thing?" The response came without hesitation: "How could you not have?" they replied, "You spoke from your heart."

No one can argue with what you feel.

In principle, stakeholders are those who have a significant stake in a particular decision; that is, they stand to win a lot, lose a lot, or they are in a position to significantly help or hinder implementation of the decision. If stakeholders don't participate in making the decision, chances are it won't be a good one.

Having all stakeholders "at the table" for decision making can be very challenging but it paves the way for smooth implementation. When stakeholders don't participate in decision making, there is a good chance they will work against decision implementing.

Practical Tip: At the outset, identify stakeholders and invite their input. For the really key stakeholders, actively encourage participation, even insist on their input.

If your group is deciding something that only some other person or group can implement, that other person or group should have an opportunity to influence the decision.

It is very helpful when stakeholders at least bless the decision-making process and agree to honor it.

In principle, when I enter into a discussion with a statement rather than a question I am presuming to already know all the answers. Most conflicts are due to misunderstanding so when my opinion is based on presumption I am probably headed for conflict.

When I begin a discussion with a question I show respect for others, that I want to hear what they have to say. The longer I remain truly open-minded the greater the chances that my opinion is based on complete understanding.

Practical Tip: Even though you might have an opinion forming in your head, hold off expressing it and start with questions instead. Be genuinely open to changing your opinion based on new things you learn. Good questions start with "why", "how" and "what." Good questions are open ended. Examples: "Why do you think that? How has it worked well in the past? What do you think is the cause of the problem?"

When I start with a question I am less threatening to others, I am more likely to develop a well-informed opinion, and I increase prospects for avoiding conflict entirely.

In principle, all stories are true and some of them really happened. Stories are kernels of truth passed on in colorful ways that help us understand the truths they contain. Most of us relate to stories much better than we relate to facts and figures. It's not so important that a story really happened but how is the story like my story, like our story? What truth does the story contain about human experience, about our nature?

Practical Tip: Make time in your group for story telling—within meetings, before and after meetings, while sharing food. Read and hear stories of other like groups, other like people. Pass on stories that ring true for you.

It is by telling and hearing stories that we come to understanding. It is by understanding that we come to good group decisions.

PS: Like most principles among these pages, I didn't make this one up. I heard it somewhere, added a little color, and passed it on.

All stories are true
and some of them really happened.

STRAW VOTE

In principle, the best group decisions are based on shared understanding of everyone's perspective, and a good way to get a quick read of where everyone stands is to take a straw vote. A straw vote is not a real vote; it doesn't count over the long run, like straw. Someone might say, "Let's just see how people feel about the latest idea. All those who tend to like it, show a thumb up. If you tend not to like it, show a thumb down. If you are neutral or undecided, show a horizontal thumb." Count the thumbs in the three categories. That's a straw vote.

It lets everyone in the group see, in a quick and general way, if the latest idea is worth more group time and energy. It also shows where the concerns are (the down thumbs) so we know who to call on to hear concerns.

Some groups use color cards for straw votes. Some use high-tech remote keypads and the results are graphed instantly on a screen in front of the room. The most efficient groups use straw votes often and with ease.

Practical Tip: Don't hesitate to call for, or participate in, a straw vote. Before calling for a straw vote, make sure the question is clear and simple; you don't want to waste group time haggling about: "What are we voting on?"

When calling for a straw vote, remind everyone that it does not count over the long run; that everyone has the right to change their mind later; that it is simply a quick and blurry snapshot of how we feel at this moment. Still, even a snapshot can be worth a thousand words.

STRENGTHS, WEAKNESSES, OPPORTUNITIES, THREATS

In principle, a look at strengths, weaknesses, opportunities, threats, referred to as a *SWOT analysis*, is an effective way to take stock of an organization or project and the context it exists in. It is often done at the start of a strategic planning process. It provides a solid foundation to build plans on.

Practical Tip: Ask the opinion of all stakeholders or at least key stakeholders—those who stand to win and lose most from the endeavor.

Ask their opinion about strengths and weaknesses, the balance sheet, what's good and bad about the organization or project. This is an internal, current look at things like financial gains and losses, assets and liabilities, staff capacity, board capacity, reputation, mission impact, etc. These are all things within our general control.

Also gather feedback on the external view, the look into the future. What opportunities and threats loom? This is a look at projected trends regarding market demand, supplies and personnel, policy and regulation, and other external factors that might affect the organization or project. To look at opportunities and threats is to assess things that we don't fully control but that we need to consider.

Take stock of your organization or project by making four lists: strengths, weaknesses, opportunities, and threats. Discuss them as a group. Good assessment is key for good strategic planning.

In principle, decision-making *structure* consists of things like rules, agendas, mandates, and plans; when these things frame our choices it frees us to focus on the substance of our work.

A third-grade teacher once explained that when she decides where the kids are to sit in the classroom this does not take away their freedom, but actually frees them from the burden of having to decide this for themselves (a potentially large burden for a third grader). It frees them to focus on math, history, and art.

Establishing a firm structure allows maximum creativity within the structure. Knowing there's a *container* provides safety and encourages risk taking. Lack of structure fosters anxiety and encourages caution. Lack of structure causes inefficiency; it requires a group to go over the same ground over and over again.

Practical Tip: Establish decision-making rules in your group and make it someone's responsibility to enforce them. Make sure everyone understands and agrees to the rules before you decide other things.

When your group takes up a complex decision, break it into pieces with a timeline for deciding each piece. Focus on one piece at a time. As you near decisions, narrow choices to a small number of alternatives.

Be bold in enforcing your structure...and go wild within it.

In principle, activities that contribute to good group decisions are not always best done by the group as a whole. Often times information, ideas, and potential solutions are all put on the table in such a tangled web that the group as a whole can't make sense of them. Other times, emotions run high in the heat of debate and cloud our ability to see clearly. Further, in the midst of lively discussion it's often hard to discern our own thoughts and feelings.

When things are confusing and the group is in disarray, we are likely to be hugely inefficient. We repeat ourselves, spin our wheels, and make clumsy progress in wrong directions.

Practical Tip: Take a break. When a group breaks for ten minutes or overnight or puts an issue to rest until the next meeting, it gives time for things to settle out and become clear. People chat informally in small groups and develop new understanding. Group facilitators have time to organize information and proposals so that others can make sense of it all. Emotions cool and personal views become clear. Time heals.

Taking a break is often the most efficient way to proceed.

TAKE A STEP

In principle, we don't need to know the whole plan in order to take the next step. To avoid a stumble we don't need to see the whole path illuminated, just the next few feet.

As if carrying a lantern through the dark, if I take just one step at a time more will be revealed. The light moves with me.

Practical Tip: Just because you can't see how everything is going to work out, don't let that stop you from taking the next step. If your group seems stuck with uncertainty, ask, "What do we need to know *just* to take the next step?" Let that be enough for now. Take a step. As an individual, let go of needing to know everything and trust that your lantern will see you through.

In principle, a simple but important decision I have to make every moment in a group is whether to open my mouth or to keep it shut, to talk or to listen. I contribute best to good group decisions if I set the default to "listen." After all, God gave me two open ears and one closeable mouth. I listen unless there are compelling reasons to talk, not vice versa.

Practical Tip: Listen most of the time. Speak up only if:

1. You personally care about the issue and have a real stake in it,

2. You understand the issue enough to add useful, accurate information,

3. No one else has already said it, even with different words, and,

4. It is the right time for speaking on the issue.

If *each* of the four conditions is met *or* if you have strong feelings just screaming to be shared then—yes!—please speak up. Others will benefit from your words. Otherwise, best to listen.

In principle, it works well when a group considers an issue three times before making a decision.

1. The first time raises notice and gets people to start thinking about the decision they are going to have to make.

2. The second time, we share information, share our interests, discuss "what if's," kick around some ideas, and perhaps develop some alternative approaches.

3. On the third consideration: decision.

Three considerations of any given issue is a satisfactory pace for most group members.

Practical Tip: When a new issue develops, formally introduce it to the group and be sure that group members know how to participate in the decision process. Give the issue or topic a name. Invite initial reactions. This is the first consideration.

Next, provide a time and place for information sharing, brainstorming, imagination, creativity, proposal development. This might be in a meeting of the full group or a committee meeting or perhaps a series of meetings. It can also happen via surveys or online collaboration. This is the second consideration.

Third, provide a time and place for final discussion and decision.

It is okay to be a bit pushy for a decision when the group has already considered the issue twice before. If the decision does not come easily on the third consideration at least decide how it is going to get decided.

In principle, when making good group decisions we try to get all the facts and fully understand before deciding. Yet it's impossible to understand every detail, every nuance, every possibility, and that's where trust takes over.

We work to understand as much as we can, but at some point we just need to trust our intuition, other people, and the process. It's called *faith*.

For the rational person, the path to resolution is mostly paved with understanding, with a bit of trust at the end. The rational person wants as much evidence as possible. For the intuitive person, the path to resolution begins with a bit of understanding and then trust paves most of the rest of the way. Going mostly on *gut feeling* is very comfortable. For all of us, truly good decisions require some combination of understanding and trust.

Practical Tip: Work on both, understanding and trust. To understand: Gather the facts, hear all perspectives, review best practices, read, apply trial and error, listen to your heart. To build trust: Do things together, eat together, demonstrate honesty and dependability, support each other through hardships, tell stories, share pictures of your loved ones.

Answer as many questions as you can but at some point you have to decide even without every answer and it comes down to trust.

In principle, understanding is that upon which we stand. It is the basis for all our beliefs and actions, like a foundation.

All that we do and say is based upon our understanding of the situation. We do best to make sure we fully understand before judging and before acting.

Practical Tip: Be aware about crossing the line between understanding the situation and solving the problem. In a conversation, ask questions before offering advice. In a meeting, be sure you fully understand the proposal before giving your opinions about it.

Ninety percent of all disagreements are the result of misunderstanding. Disagreements often disappear when we take the time to understand where each other are coming from, how things look from other points of view.

Misunderstandings, presumptions, and premature judgments almost always result in bad decisions. Shared understanding is the basis for creative, peaceful, enduring decisions.

Ninety percent of all disagreements
are the result of misunderstanding.

In principle, the most likely path for a group to be highly productive, happy, and endure over generations is for individuals to put group needs over individual needs.

In western culture we receive many messages that encourage us to put self first, the most likely path to short term gain. In a *me-first* culture individuals prevail but groups, communities, and species die. Good group decisions require an attitude of *us over me*.

Practical Tip: In group decision making, be thoughtful about how a decision affects the group as a whole. Whatever would be best for the group, work on that path, vote that way. Consider impacts of decisions on other groups, communities, and species; and into the future. Apply humility.

*Whatever would be best for the group,
work on that path, vote that way.*

In principle, in order to move from one topic to the next we have to have a next topic. Without something else important to do, there is little incentive to change what we are doing.

Strategic plans and meeting agendas are lists of next topics. The meeting facilitator moves the group forward by reminding them of the other important topics to be discussed. It's not that we want to end this topic because we don't care about it; it's just that we need to start the next one.

If you or your group is in a negative place emotionally, the best medicine is often a healthy distraction.

Practical Tip: Have a next step always in mind. Make plans and agendas. Set group and personal development goals.

The skilled meeting facilitator and the effective leader know what's next and are always prepared to go the next step. One need not always take the next step but, if one is prepared, at least it's an option. Without a next step, we're stuck.

Without something else important to do,
there is little incentive to change what we are doing.

WHAT'S THE PROBLEM?

In principle, more often than not, a group will develop a great solution to the wrong problem. Before proceeding with a solution we need to see that it is aimed at the problem, and to do that we need to bring the problem into focus. Taking time to define the problem may seem annoying and unnecessary in the short term, but can save huge amounts of time and energy over the long run.

Defining the problem as a group also checks our shared expectations. It helps me decide, "Is this something that I want to participate in?"

Practical Tip: Before discussing solutions, discuss the problem. What are we trying to fix? What is the specific scope of the problem that we are willing to take on? How would we know if the problem were fixed? Are we the right group to fix it?

On paper, write something like, "The problem is that _____."
It could be a sentence or it could be a paragraph.

Refrain from discussing solutions until you have agreement on the problem statement. Make sure that all those working on the problem are aware of the written problem statement and agree with it.

Before firing off solutions, make sure the problem is squarely in your sights.

In principle, the value of written words is that several people can see them simultaneously and that they endure over time. Written words anchor specific events, ideas, perspectives, decisions.

Further, the process of choosing words helps us be sure that we understand. Writing and agreeing on words together forces our shared understanding.

Without a written record to underpin the understanding or agreement, we can count on ever-changing accounts of what happened.

Practical Tip: When making group decisions, write down words to represent the decisions. You might write words on a flip chart or computer screen for all to see and clarify in the moment, or you might write them for later clarification in the form of meeting minutes (written notes of a meeting). Many groups circulate draft minutes, invite corrections, and then formally approve a final version.

Agreeing on written words is harder than just nodding approval of spoken words, but it saves confusion and conflict over the long run.

NOTES

[1] "1987-2000 Warmest Year on Record," United Nations World Meteorological Organization, December 13, 2007. Press release.

[2] IUCN Red List of Threatened Species, "State of the World's Species, 2008," International Union for Conservation of Nature, http://cmsdata.iucn.org/downloads/state_of_the_world_s_species_factsheet_en.pdf (accessed July 16, 2009).

[3] Dirk Bryant, Daniel Nielsen and Laura Tangley, *Last Frontier Forests: Ecosystems and Economies on the Edge* (Washington D.C.: World Resources Institute, 1997).

[4] "30 Wars Greet the 2008 'Day of Global Ceasefire,'" Project Ploughshares: September 18, 2008. Press release.

[5] Kevin Watkins et al, *Human Development Report 2007/2008,* (New York: United Nations Development Programme, 2009).

[6] Joanna Macy, "The Great Turning," Center for Ecoliteracy, 2007.

[7] David C. Korten, *The Great Turning* (Bloomfield, CT: Kumarian Press, Inc. and San Francisco, CA: Berrett-Koehler Publishers, Inc., 2006).

[8] Earth Charter Commission, "The Earth Charter" (Paris, France: United Nations Educational, Scientific and Cultural Organization, 2000).

[9] Ibid.

[10] United Nations General Assembly "Report of the United Nations Conference on Environment and Development", United Nations General Assembly, http://www.un.org/documents/ga/conf151/aconf15126-1annex1.htm (accessed July 2009).

[11] Alfie Kohn, *No Contest: The Case Against Competition* (Boston: Houghton Mifflin, 1986).

[12] Bob Dylan, "A Hard Rain's A-Gonna Fall," Special Rider Music, 1963.

[13] David Kouzes and Barry Posner, *The Leadership Challenge*, 4th Edition (San Francisco, CA: Jossey-Bass, 2007).

TIPS BY TOPIC

ATTITUDE AND PERSONAL GROWTH

Act as If	Kindness	Not her Fault, her Type
Credit the Group	Leadership	Okay to Change Your
Earth Community	Love	Mind
Free from Past	Mistakes	Speak Your Truth and
Good in Everyone	Moral Compass	Let Go
Gratitude	More Wagging...	Take a Step
Humility	My Part	Trust Takes Over
Indifference	Not All About Money	Us Over Me

COMMUNICATION

Criticism Private	Do What You Say	On Behalf Cautions
Demonstrate Listening	E-mail	Reflective Pause
Difference between	Good Information...	Start with a Question
Launch and Land	Listen	Talk or Listen
Direct Communication	No Complaining...	Written Words Clarify

CONFLICT PREVENTION

Assumptions Lead to	Contain Disagreement	Resentments have
Trouble	Enforcement	Roots in
At Home and Families	Interests rather than	Expectations
Best Solutions Begin	Positions	Revenge is Never a
with Self	Lose Now, Win Later	Reason
Causes of Conflict...	Morality as Agreed	Rules First
Change or Accept	My First Thought...	Understanding First
Conflict Resolution...	Outside Issues	What's the Problem?

CREATIVITY

Agenda Setting Access	Freedom of Speech	Stories
Alternative Solutions	No One Dominates	Structure Sets You
Different Views	Outside Influence	Free
Feedback Please	Recreation	Take a Break

EFFICIENCY

Agreements Stand...	Hands Off	Name Leads
Changing the Process...	Just Enough	Opt Out
Flat for Planning...	Know Your Lines	Orientation
Get a Second	Let Things Die	Stakeholders...

GROUP TECHNIQUE

Carrots are Better...	Hot Hand	Shared Values
Committees	Inauguration	Shared Vision...
Consensus at the Core	Incrementally	Small Goals
Decide How to Decide	Loose in the Harness	Straw Vote
Define the Edges	Measure to Manage	Strengths,
Direction more	Multi-Vote	Weaknesses...
Important than Pace	Okay to Change Plans	Three Times
Facilitation	and Rules	Considered
Ground Rules	Plan, Meet, Write Up	What's Next?

INDEX

mistakes, utility of, 73
misunderstandings
    fostered by e-mail, 44
    as source of conflict, 26, 30, 113
modeling the way, 66
money, in group decisions, 83
moral compass, 74
morale, low, 100
morality
    as agreed, 75
    universal, 74
morals, knowing one's own and the
    group's, 86
motions, seconding of, 51
motivation, prodded by outside influ-
    ence, 90
moving the bar down, 100
multiple consideration, 111
multi-voting, 77
Myers-Briggs personality assessment,
    84
"my part," 14, 24, 79

nature, human, 104
nature, respect for, 74
needs, individual, subordinated to
    group needs, 114
negative comments, 47
negative emotions, 43
next step, 109, 115
    small vs. big, 60
next topics, 115
noncompliance, with group decisions
    and rules, 45, 54

objective, determination of, prior to
    action, 41
oil consumption, 9
on-behalf speech and action, 87
one on one
    conversation, saving group energy,
        28
    time with new members, 89
on-line surveys, 77
"open forum" in meetings, 19
open-mindedness, 58, 103
openness to listening, reciprocated, 68
opinions
    of all stakeholders, in SWOT analysis,
        106

based on understanding elicited by
    questions, 103
minority, 50
opportunity
    assessing, 106
    to participate, equal, 97
optimism, 6, 54, 76
    and envisioning better things, 25
opting out, 88
organization, benefits to, of group deci-
    sion making, 12–13
orientation of new members, 89
outside influence, 90
outside issues, 91
over-fixing, 63
ownership
    lingering, 33
    of own errors, 33
    relinquishing, 33, 58

pace, direction more important than, 41
participation, equal opportunity for, 97
passion, nurturing in others, 66, 71
past, freedom from, 49
past performance, as benchmark, 72
pauses and breaks, 31, 108
    recreational, 93
    reflective, 94
peace
    boycott as tool of, 88
    in decision making, 18, 97, 113
    and detachment, 101
    and disagreement, 32
    and extra-financial impacts of deci-
        sions, 83
    global, 11, 18, 23 (see also war)
    and love for neighbors, 71
    not to be gained by harming others,
        96
    personal, 13
    through shared understanding, 37
peacemakers, 18
peace seeker, inner, 64
penalties, appropriate, for rule viola-
    tions, 45
performance, past, 72
personality types, 84, 112
pictures of loved ones, sharing, 112
"piece of the puzzle" model, 39
pilot projects, 60
planning, 107

vs. implementation, 4
long-term, and large group decision
    making, 48
for meetings, 92
strategic, process for, 106
plans, changes in, 85
policy
    changes in, *vs.* individual change, 24
    high-level, and large group decision
        making, 48
politicians, and deciding how to decide,
    35
positioned knowing, 4, 7, 13–14, 39
positions, *vs.* interests, 62
positive comments, 47
Posner, Barry, 66
power sharing, 19
praise, 25
prematurely stated positions, 62
preparedness, for meetings, 92
presumptions, 113
priorities, multi-voting to reduce list of,
    77
private criticism, 34
problems
    defining, 21, 116
    need for full understanding before
        solving, 113
process
    change in, rarely the solution, 28
    control of, in non-collaborative mod-
        els, 7
    at expense of substance, 67
    as framework for changing plans or
        rules, 85
    manipulated in procedural debate,
        46
    need to challenge, 66
    role of facilitator, 46
    strategic planning, 106
    from substance, 7–8
profit, and short-term selfish impact, 83
program committees, 29
progress, incremental, 60
    trust in, 109
proposals
    bold, 36
    development of, 97, 111
provocative, value of being, 36
public criticism, 34
puzzle, at least two pieces to every, 79

quantifiable goals, 72
question, starting with a, 103
quick results, group urge for, 41

raising notice, 111
rational person, *vs.* intuitive, 112
recess, 93
recreation, 93
reference group, 72
regulation and policies, external, as-
    sessment of, 106
relationships, long-term, not to be sacri-
    ficed to short-term decisions, 70
relevant experiences, outside influences
    with, 90
repeated voting rounds, 77
resentments, 20, 33
    roots of, in expectations, 95
respect
    for all people, 74 (*see also* good in
        everyone)
    group culture of, 87
    for nature, 74 (*see also* environmen-
        tal values)
    shown by starting with question, 103
respectful disagreement, 32
revenge, 32, 49, 96
Robert's Rules of Order, 6, 51
role, knowing one's, 65
rules, 107
    changes in, 85
    of engagement, 97
    legitimate crafting of, 45
    preceding action, 97
    violations of, 45, 55, 97
    See also ground rules

sadness, over dying things, 67
sarcasm, and e-mail, 44
scope of problem, group capacity for,
    116
screen, computer, display of written
    word on, 117
script, following *vs.* departures from, 85
seating plans, 35, 107
second, obtaining a, 51
security, for meeting participants, 92
seeing things differently, acceptance as,
    27

ORDER MORE COPIES

Get more copies of *The Wisdom of Group Decisions* through your local bookstore or at our website where we offer significant discounts for multiple copies.

Get a copy for everyone in your group.

COMMENT, VOTE, SUGGEST, SUBSCRIBE

At our website, comment on the principles and tips in this book and several others that Craig Freshley has written. Check out the comments of others. Vote for your favorites. Suggest your own ideas for new principles and tips. Sign up to receive new principles and tips by e-mail every two weeks for free.

We would love to hear from you.

www.GoodGroupDecisions.com

Breinigsville, PA USA
26 September 2010
246083BV00001B/24/P